RUNNING ON EMPTY

Life Lessons to Refuel Your Faith

RUNNING
ON EMPTY

Life Lessons to Refuel Your Faith

ARRON CHAMBERS

LIFE JOURNEY®

Bringing Home the Message for Life

COOK COMMUNICATIONS MINISTRIES
Colorado Springs, Colorado • Paris, Ontario
KINGSWAY COMMUNICATIONS LTD
Eastbourne, England

Life Journey® is an imprint of
Cook Communications Ministries, Colorado Springs, CO 80918
Cook Communications, Paris, Ontario
Kingsway Communications, Eastbourne, England

RUNNING ON EMPTY
© 2005 by Arron Chambers

First Printing, 2005
Printed in the United States of America
1 2 3 4 5 6 7 8 9 10 Printing/Year 09 08 07 06 05

Cover Design: TrueBlue Design/Sandy Flewelling
Cover Photo: Corbis®

To contact the author, please visit www.arronchambers.com.

Library of Congress Cataloging-in-Publication Data

Chambers, Arron.
  Running on empty : life lessons to refuel your faith / by Arron
Chambers.
    p. cm.
  Includes bibliographical references.
  ISBN 1-56292-304-8 (pbk.)
  1. Christian life. I. Title.
  BV4501.3.C43 2005
  248.4--dc22
                        2004030814

For my wife, Rhonda.
Because of Christ I will have life in heaven.
Because of you I have heaven in this life.

CONTENTS

ACKNOWLEDGMENTS

The book you are holding in your hands was a dream I held in my heart for many years. This book would still be only a dream if it were not for the following people:

My wife, Rhonda, and my children, Ashton, Levi, Sylas, and Payton—Thanks for your love and support. I treasure each moment we spend together. God is so good.

My parents, Roger and Linda Chambers—You are my heroes. You created in me a passion for God and a passion for life. I am who I am because of you. Dad, I miss you. Mom, I cherish you. All my love.

My sisters and their husbands: Leigh-Angela and Jeff Holbrook and Leslie and Shan Wood; my brother and his wife: Adam and Patricia Chambers—I love you so much. It's great to be together.

John and Mary Smith, my parents-in-law—Ordinary names, extraordinary people. Thank you for caring for my wife and kids while I finished this book. I love you very much, Mom and Dad.

Dr. Ben Lerner—Thank you for believing in and investing in my dream. You've adjusted more than my back, and I will always be grateful.

Rusty Fischer—Thank you for all you did to get this book published. Your guidance and editorial suggestions as I began this project are the biggest reasons this book is a reality today. I will always be grateful to you. You're the best.

Tamela Hancock Murray, my agent—Thank you for believing in me. Your encouragement and eternal optimism kept me motivated throughout this project. I'm so blessed to be represented by you.

Mary McNeil, my editor; Michele Tennesen, my publicist; Diane Gardner; Phyllis Williams; and the team at Cook Communications—It's an honor to be working with such a wonderful ministry and such Christ-like people. Thank you for being so professional, patient, and kind.

Twila Sias—Thank you for investing so much time in this book teaching me about parallel structure, tenses, and dangling modifiers, but I want to thank you more for investing so much time in me. You are my Barnabas, my mentor, and my friend.

Mark Atteberry—Thank you for all you did to help me during this project. Your advice and encouragement mean more to me than you can know.

Andrew and Jamie Peterson—Your friendship is so important to me and my family.

Mark and Lori Smith, Dave and Jan Smith, Phil and Tonia Smith—Thank you for not telling me when you were sick of hearing about this book. You are so dear to me, and I'm honored to be your brother-in-law. I love you.

President Bob Wetzel and the library staff at Emmanuel School of Religion—Thank you for being so generous with your facilities during the final weeks of this project. Your seminary *is* beautiful inside and out.

Terry and Tammy Davis—Thanks for silent football, *Jumpstart Your Brain*, homemade pizza, urban legends, SAK, and the years of friendship. Your creative input added value to this project and effectiveness to my ministry.

My Leadership Team at Southside Christian Church: Travis Jacob, Eli Reyes, Olivia Padgett, Melissa Clark, Darrell Portwood, Kenny Funk, Steve Long, and Randy Patterson—it would have been impossible to finish this book without your support and encouragement. It's such an honor and joy to serve God with you. I love you deeply. May God continue to pour out his blessings on us as we seek to help people in Central Florida to "Get A Life" through Christ Jesus our Lord.

My family at Southside Christian Church—Your faith, optimism, flexibility, joy, love, and support mean more to me than you could ever know. My time ministering with you has been a glimpse of heaven on earth. I love you very much.

INTRODUCTION

I have come that they may have life, and have it to the full.

—John 10:10

I ran out of gas once. I was shocked. My '89 Topaz had numerous problems, but I assumed the gas gauge was not one of them. The gauge clearly told me that I had enough gas to reach my destination, but for some reason—despite what my gauge told me—I found myself stranded on the side of the road.

I felt stupid. I felt so betrayed, so humiliated. "I can't be out of gas!" I yelled out loud.

The gauge *said* I had a full tank.

As I walked down the highway past the gravel, tire parts, and road kill, I mentally vented my anger: *That stupid fuel gauge.* I felt a little better as I blamed an inanimate object for my predicament.

Everyone else was zipping happily by me in cars with obviously functioning fuel gauges. My fuel gauge deceived me and I was stuck.

It's not fun to run out of gas.

Have you ever run out of gas?

Not your car—*you.*

I have.

The gauge I was looking at in my life clearly read *full*, but I still found myself stranded on the side of life's road. The gauge I was using—the *world*—was flawed, but I didn't realize it until my tank was empty and I was going nowhere. If we judge whether or not our lives are "full" based on the world's standards, we are destined to run out of gas.

The problem is that the world says our lives are full simply because we are busy.

My wife and I spent the summer after our college graduation traveling. We drove thousands of miles seeing the country and visiting family. One of our final stops was in the booming metropolis of Sugar Tree Ridge, Ohio, where we stayed on my wife's grandparents' farm. That evening we enjoyed a delicious dinner of fried chicken, fresh green beans, homemade biscuits, and strawberry shortcake. As we sat there with Mamaw and Papaw Emery delighting in the taste of the food and the sweetness of the fellowship, I told Mamaw how much I liked the chicken. Then she said something that changed my life forever.

She thanked me, then revealed that the chicken I was enjoying had been enjoying its own life just hours earlier. Mamaw Emery made chicken the old-fashioned way—she caught it!

I sat quietly and grew queasy as she explained in detail how she caught the chicken, stepped on its neck, and pulled its head off.

The story got better.

I was sitting with a half-chewed piece of chicken hanging out of my mouth—unsure I wanted to swallow—as she continued the vivid description of the gentle way she prepared our main course.

Mamaw explained that after she separated the chicken's neck from its body, the body flapped frantically around the yard. Fun. I carefully swallowed—thanking Mamaw for teaching me an important lesson—and then excused myself from the table.

Several years after that meal, as I thought about that chicken running around with its head cut off, I realized that Mamaw Emery really had taught me an important lesson: activity does not equal vitality.[1]

Just because we are *busy* doesn't mean that we are *alive*.

Just because the world says our lives are full doesn't mean that our lives *really* are full. Our lives are not full simply because we are working hard, playing hard, and living hard. When we try to fill our lives with the fuel of this world, we find ourselves running on empty.

I want you to let true Life—Jesus Christ—help you have a truly full life.

The gospel of John records that Jesus said, "I have come that they may have life, and have it to the full" (John 10:10). In other words, Christ said that he wants us to have "life—in abundance." He wants our tanks full of life, life, and more life spilling over us, through us, and out of us.

The apostle John loved life. He used a form of the word *life* sixty-nine times in his gospel. He was not alone in this passion. Luke talked about life thirty-two times, Matthew twenty-nine times, and Mark thirteen times.

John, however, talked about life more than twice as much as any one of the other gospel writers. Why was he obsessed with life? We know that he was one of Jesus' closest friends—so close that while on the cross, Jesus entrusted John with the care of his mother.

I think John was obsessed with life lived in abundance because he walked with the very source of life for more than three years.

I read that every person over the age of thirty-three is obsessed with death. Death will inevitably arrive for each of us, but first we must live.

I want to be obsessed with life.

Jesus was and is obsessed with life. He didn't come so that our lives would be busy. He came so that our lives would be *full*.

I want to have an abundant life—as Jesus defined it. And I want the same for you. In this book, we will journey with Jesus through the gospel of John, identifying with Christ the twenty-one elements of an abundant life. As we incorporate these principles into our lives, we'll discover how meaningful an abundant life can be.

One of my favorite movies is *Braveheart*. It is the story of a Scottish rebel, William Wallace, who led an uprising against the cruel English ruler Edward "Longshanks" who wanted the crown of Scotland for himself. After Wallace's wife is killed, he begins a long quest to make Scotland free, once and for all. Near the end of the movie, Wallace is visited in his prison cell by the daughter of the king, who has fallen in love with him. He is to be executed, and she enters his cell to beg him to confess and swear allegiance to the King of England. Wallace will not compromise; he will not surrender. The princess, knowing there is no hope for Wallace unless he confesses, says, "You will die! It will be awful!" To which Wallace replies, "Every man dies, not every man really lives."

That quote leaves me feeling both convicted and motivated. Conviction comes when we ask ourselves, *Am I truly living?* Motivation comes when we embrace the conviction our answer brings.

Are we truly living? We get up; brush our teeth; hug our kids; and go to work, school, or to the couch. We inhale and exhale shallow, safe breaths. We pay our bills. We confront a multitude of stimuli throughout the day. But is this living?

It's time for us to get a life.

Maybe you've only heard this challenge from a critic: "You think you'll get that promotion? Get a life!" "You think he's being faithful to you? Get a life!" "You're going back to college? Get a life!" "You're going to start going back to church? Get a life!"

I want to steal this challenge from the critic and give it to you with a smile on my face and with joyful anticipation for you if you accept my challenge: Get a life!

Each day of life is a gift. Take it, say thanks, and open it. Lift the corner of the box and try to imagine the treasure waiting for you inside. Tear it open. Rip away the stuff of this earth and gaze at the present from heaven.

Get a life!

Don't get sucked into the routine of the dead: waking, working, eating, sleeping, paying, and dying. Dream big dreams. Inhale and exhale deeply. As often as possible, skip.

My daughter is a great skipper. She skips everywhere.

Do you know why she skips? She skips because she doesn't have to pay taxes. She skips because all her friends are still alive. She skips because she's healthy. She skips because she's glad to be alive. Have you ever seen a sad skipper? Skipping is a sign of a joy-filled heart.

We all need to stop whatever we're doing that we think is so important and skip.

(Side note: I think that we could use a little more skipping in this world. I say we get all the world leaders, put them in one room, and say, "We're going to talk politics, but first … everyone skip!" I think this has real potential.)

We need to sing songs, smell the flowers, hug our kids, stay up late, laugh excessively, call an old friend, and kiss our spouse—on the lips—like we did before our hair started falling out or turning gray.

Get a life! We are the children of the Lord of Life. To not live fully each day—to waste one moment of life—would be to deny our identity and squander an opportunity.

My sister wrote a song with a profoundly true line. "Time's like a bubble that's caught on the breeze. You reach out to touch it—and it's gone."[2]

I just turned thirty-four and I can't believe how quickly I got here. Time flies whether or not one is having fun. As I blew out my candles, I felt convicted. What had I done in thirty-four years? I also felt motivated and decided—at that very moment—to write this book. I will not let thirty-five arrive without writing the book I've said for years I'd write.

I have three humble goals for this book. First, I want it to be practical. It's full of simple stories and images designed to be remembered easily and woven into the fabric of your daily life. Second, I want you to be blessed in some way for having read it. Your time is precious and should not be wasted. Third, I want every person who reads this book to remember—if only for a moment—that life is a special gift to be cherished, opened, and enjoyed.

I am a simple person, so this is a simple book with short chapters, uncomplicated themes, and down-to-earth lessons. There are twenty-one chapters in the gospel of John; each presents elements of a truly full life, so there are twenty-one chapters in this book.

I am also a practical person, so throughout this book you'll find sections titled "Refuel!" which are easy activities designed to get you out of your comfort zone and into life.

Walk slowly through this book. Linger in its pages. Reflect on its stories. Read a chapter. Walk away. Take a nap. Take a run. Pet the dog. Kick the cat. (Just making sure you're paying attention.) Lie on your back in the front yard and see what amazing creatures are hiding in the clouds. Come back to this book before you go to bed. As much as possible, try to integrate the lessons of this book into your everyday life.

And when our journey together is through, look me up so we can talk about what it is to get a life. You won't have any trouble spotting me. I'll be the one skipping.

Arron Chambers

www.arronchambers.com

LIGHT

In him was life, and that life was the light of men.
The light shines in the darkness, but the darkness has not understood it.

—John 1:4–5

I was afraid of the dark when I was a little kid.

One Saturday morning, I woke before the sun came up. I wanted a drink of water, so I began to crawl out of my bunk bed when—to my horror—I encountered the most hideous creature I had ever seen hulking to gargantuan proportions just beyond the door.

Well ... I didn't actually *see* the creature. I saw its grotesque shadow on the wall outside my room. I was petrified. As I lay in bed with my covers clinched in my tightly curled fingers, I could see the monster's movements reflecting on the wall. I couldn't yell—he surely would enter my room immediately and devour me just to keep me quiet. I couldn't move—he would hear me and eat my entire family. So I lay there staring at the wall outside my room.

I don't know how long I lay in the dark, afraid of the monster, but I do know how he died.

As the sun rose that morning, the monster on the wall began to disappear. My fear faded away with the light of day. With the rising of the sun, I realized that the monster on the wall wasn't a monster at all. It was the moonlit shadow of a plant outside my window dancing on the hallway wall. I was still thirsty, so I bravely jumped out of bed and got my drink.

Darkness will make a thirsty boy so afraid that he will not walk ten steps to get a drink of water.

In the darkness we have more shadows than substance.

In the darkness we have more questions than answers.

In the darkness we have more fear than faith.

In the darkness we have more fantasy than reality.

In the darkness Satan likes to put shadows of monsters on the walls to paralyze us with fear.

I'm not afraid of the dark anymore, but I still don't like it. I'm in good company, too. God doesn't like the dark either.

God's first *spoken* words in the Bible were, "Let there be light" (Gen. 1:3). God created light first because it is essential for life. John reminds us that Jesus was there when God turned the lights on for the first time so that we could have life. "Through him all things were made; without him nothing was made that has been made. In him was life, and that life was the light of men" (John 1:3–4).

God's first *living* Word in this world was Jesus, "the true light" (John 1:9). God sent light to our dark world because the Light is essential for life. Light was the first element of life on earth, and it's the first element of a life that is truly full. Just as we need light to live in this world, we need the "Light of the World" (John 8:12) to live life abundantly. No light—no life. Know light—know life.

Light is the first element of a full life.

There are creatures that thrive in the darkness and have developed a comfortable existence in a world separated from light: lightning bugs, owls, rats, vampires, and Pharisees.

Nicodemus was a creature of the dark. He even came to Jesus at night, presumably so he would not be seen by others (see John 3:2). As a Pharisee, Nicodemus was a ruler of the Jews and a distinguished scholar. We know from John 3 that he was also interested in the ministry of the Light of the World. His world was a dark world of cold religious traditions and rituals.

Cave-dwelling animals that live in the dark become blind and pale. Like a cave-dwelling creature, Nicodemus was spiritually blind and pale. He was comfortable in the dark, and so it is fitting that his first encounter with Jesus was in the dark.

Mine was. I was trapped in the darkness of sin when I first embraced the Light of Life.

God designed our eyes to adjust to different amounts of light. When we first leave the bright light and enter a dark room, we can't see. We bend over, stretch out our arms, and try to keep from kicking a toe on something hard, but eventually we adjust quite well to the dark. In fact, we can grow comfortable there.

Are you comfortable in the darkness? Bars are dark. Back-alleys are dark. Night clubs are dark. It's ironic that it's called "Night-*Life*" when, in fact, so much of what occurs when the sun is blocked and the lights are off is so spiritually deadly. Darkness hides sin; it will kill us if we try to live there too long.

When you've been in a dark room long enough for your eyes to adjust to the darkness, light is painful and disruptive. Turn on the lights in a dark room filled with people and you'll hear the moans of frustration. The immediate impact of bright

 ## Refuel!

1. Grab a flashlight, go into a room, and turn out the lights.

2. Read John 1 and then turn out the flashlight.

3. In the darkness of that closet, confess the darkness in your life.

4. When you are finished, turn on the light.

5. Repeat when necessary.

light piercing into darkness is discomfort, but the long-term impact is life. That light and the life it brings are vital.

Turn the light on.

A country church was located so remotely that for many years there was no electricity. Finally, an enterprising company offered electricity to the area. At one of the business meetings of the church, someone stood and said, "Now that we have electricity, I make a motion that our church buys a chandelier."

The most cantankerous member of the church, who always voted "agin" what everyone else was for, made the following plea: "I hope we don't vote to buy a chandelier. After thinking long and hard on this situation, I have come up with three reasons why we should forget about buying a chandelier. In the first place, if we bought a chandelier, nobody would know how to spell it. In the second place, nobody in this church knows how to play it. And, besides all that, what we need is some light!"

We need light, too. If you are living in a world of darkness, then you are living in a world of death. If you want to live an abundant life, then you must be committed to live in the light. Leave the dark thinking behind. Leave the dark living behind.

In the dark you can't see.

In the dark you can get hurt.

In the dark you will deteriorate.

In the dark you will die.

God created us for light, and he sent the Light to create life for us in this life and in the next, so "Let there be light!"

There. That ought to take care of the monsters.

PURITY

He did not need man's testimony about man, for he knew what was in a man.

—*John 2:25*

I love Campbell's broccoli and cheese soup. One night when my wife was out of town—and before kids necessitated eating healthy meals with food from all the food groups—I found myself hungry and wanting something quick for dinner.

I went to the cupboard and selected a nice clean can of broccoli and cheese soup. I turned the stove on, prepared a sleeve of saltine crackers, carefully positioned the bowl and spoon, and began to open a can of my favorite soup.

Suddenly, I was horrified and no longer hungry. Careful removal of the sharp-edged lid revealed a type of blackness I'd never seen before. I instantly realized the soup had gone bad and turned from a lovely off-white color to a disgusting shade of greenish black garnished with a couple of pieces of hair!

I lost my appetite.

God has no stomach for impurity, either. Why? His Glory.

In John 2, we are exposed to the glory of God in Christ when Jesus performed his first and second miracles. His first miracle was changing water into wine at a wedding in Cana. His second miracle—one that took much longer—was changing a group of Galilean vagabonds into a group of faithful disciples willing to follow him, worship him, and live for him.

⬕ REFUEL!

1. Go to the cupboard (or the grocery store) and get two cans of broccoli and cheese soup.
2. Set the cans on the kitchen table, sit down, and read the second chapter of John.
3. Open one of the cans, look inside, thank God for purity, and then enjoy a bowl of soup.
4. Keep a can handy as a reminder to be pure.

John explained how the second miracle of Cana occurred: "This, the first of his miraculous signs, Jesus performed at Cana in Galilee. He thus revealed his *glory,* and his disciples put their faith in him" (John 2:11). God's glory is transformational.

On this occasion, God chose to transform his disciples by revealing his glory through a miracle. At other times, God chose to transform people by revealing his glory in the place where they worshiped him: his temple.

After Solomon completed the temple, the Israelite priests saw the glory of God and stopped in the middle of the service (see 1 Kings 8:11; 2 Chron. 5:14; 7:2). Shortly afterward, when all the Israelites saw the glory of the Lord fill the temple, they knelt on the pavement with their faces to the ground and worshiped … saying that God was "good" (see 2 Chron. 7:1–3). Isaiah also saw the glory of God in the temple and was transformed, crying, "I am ruined! For I am a man of unclean lips" (Isa. 6:5). Ezekiel saw the glory of God filling the temple, as well, and fell facedown (see Ezek. 1:28).

Do you want to know something interesting? No one else would see the glory of the Lord filling the temple for almost seven hundred years. And guess who finally saw God's glory filling the temple again. The apostle John.[1]

Seven hundred years is a long time for the temple to be glory-less.

Jesus wanted his temple to be filled with God's glory, but found it filled with impurity instead. It had become a marketplace. During the Passover, Jews came from everywhere to worship God and find forgiveness of their sins by offering animal sacrifices at the temple.

Typically, the worshipers would bring their best animals from home to be sacrificed for their worst sins at God's holy temple. Christ found something different on this visit to his temple. He found lazy worshipers buying less-than-average but convenient animals sold by unscrupulous vendors in his Father's house—and he got angry.

This was not their house—it was his Father's house.

This was not worship—it was desecration.

Jesus had no appetite for what he found inside the temple.

It was time to clean house.

It was time for the temple to be filled with the glory of God once more. Jesus made a whip, drove out the money changers, purified his temple, and filled it with the glory of God again.

You and I are temples, too.

The apostle Paul wrote, "Do you not know that your body is a temple of the Holy Spirit, who is in you, whom you have received from God? You are not your own; you were bought at a price. Therefore honor God with your body" (1 Cor. 6:19–20).

Our bodies are not our own—they are a temple of the Holy Spirit, and like the temple, our bodies are to be used to honor God.

Do our temples need to be cleaned out, too?

We learn at least four important lessons from this first example of "spring cleaning" that will help us to get a life.

1. JESUS DOESN'T LIKE IMPURITY.

Sin makes God angry. Jesus was angry that people who should have known better were doing something that was obviously wrong and deadly. His anger was evident to the money changers and to his disciples, and it is evident to us today. The apostle Paul warned us that the only thing that comes from sin is death (see Rom. 6:23)—not pleasure, not happiness, not fulfillment, and not popularity. Death. This is why Christ was so angry. He didn't see innocent people making money. He saw sinful people dying. Sin was stealing their lives.

Are we doing things that make God angry?

Are we busy with things that only bring death?

God wants us to nurture life.

2. JESUS HAS INTENSE PASSION FOR HIS TEMPLE.

Sin can't be ignored. Jesus couldn't ignore what he saw because he was consumed with "zeal" for the temple (John 2:17). He did not want his temple to be permanently destroyed by humans.

Do you know that God has zeal for your life, too? We are his temple, and Jesus does not want us permanently destroyed by sin. He will not sit by and ignore our sin. He will rise up and deal with it because he wants us to "Get a Life."

3. JESUS WILL DO WHATEVER IT TAKES TO CLEAN THE TEMPLE.

Sin is deadly. In this situation, Jesus made a whip, flipped tables, and physically drove the impurity out. In fewer than three years, however, he would do something even more drastic. He would die on a cross to pay the wages of our sin. And this sacrifice was on his mind while he cleansed the temple.

As his whip was hitting the tables, he was thinking about the whip that would be hitting his back. As he drove out the animals being sold for sacrifice, he was thinking about the sacrifice that would drive out our sin. As his authority was questioned by sinners, he was thinking about the authority we would gain through the shedding of his blood.

How do we know that he was thinking about his death while cleansing his temple? In the midst of the cleansing, Jesus said, "Destroy this temple, and I will raise it again in three days" (John 2:19).

The Jews in the temple didn't get it. They thought he was talking about the physical temple. "It has taken forty-six years to build this temple, and you are going to raise it in three days?" (John 2:20). The disciples didn't get it either until after Jesus rose from the dead. John honestly admitted this when he wrote, "After he was raised from the dead, his disciples recalled what he had said. Then they believed the Scripture and the words that Jesus had spoken" (John 2:22).

I hope we get it.

4. JESUS ALREADY KNOWS WHAT'S IN OUR TEMPLE.

Sin can't be hidden; it shouldn't be hidden.

John wrote, "He did not need man's testimony about man, for he knew what was in a man" (John 2:25). Jesus knows what's inside us, and he wants us to know how dangerous the things that are inside us can be.

On July 1, 1998, *USA Today* carried a story that illustrates this truth. When the city fathers of Echo, Oregon, a community of 615 people, decided it was time to remodel city hall, workers ventured into the 4,000-square-foot attic and found five tons of pigeon droppings. The mess had collected there since the two-story building opened in 1916. "It's a wonder the ceiling didn't collapse," city manager Diane Berry said. Even with a high-efficiency vacuum and several shovels, it took five days to clean the attic.

Jesus already knows what's in our attic, and we are foolish if we think we can hide it from him.

He knows about the anger.

He knows about the greed.

He knows about the pride.

He knows about the lies.

He knows about the lust.

He knows about the selfishness.

We can't hide anything from him, so let's not even try.

After the apostle Paul wrote about the wages of sin, he also wrote, "but the gift of God is eternal life in Christ Jesus our Lord" (Rom. 6:23).

Jesus wants us to live an eternal and abundant life. He wants to open the door to our temple and find purity. He wants to stroll through our temple and see life. He was dying for us to know this.

NEWNESS

I tell you the truth, no one can see the kingdom of God unless he is born again.

—*John 3:3*

Childbirth is messy ... but necessary.

I've been blessed to witness the birth of all my children. I found myself in an emotional vortex each time as I watched my wife experience so much anxiety, pain, and joy. I'll never forget the tidal wave of emotions that swept over me while seeing my children for the first time when they made their entrance (or should it be exit?) into this world. I cried every time.

I even cry when strangers have babies. I cry almost every time I watch *A Baby Story* on The Learning Channel. Childbirth is an amazing, exciting, and hopeful thing. Carl Sandburg said, "A baby is God's opinion that life should go on." Each birth is a new beginning.

Now, some people claim to remember their birth, but I honestly doubt it. (I have a hard time remembering what my wife asked me to do thirteen minutes ago.) I don't remember my birth, but I don't doubt it. I know it happened. This simple fact brings purpose to life. We are born for a reason and grow with high expectations from on high.

God expects big things from us as we grow. He expects us to mature and to gain wisdom. He expects us to become more self-less and giving. He expects us to love. He expects us to live.

He does not, however, expect us to grow old. Yes, we'll age, but that doesn't mean we have to be old.

Being old is not about age; it's about attitude.

God doesn't like old things; he likes new things. In his book, he inspired the following thoughts about old things:

> For we know that our *old* self was crucified with him so that the body of sin might be done away with, that we should no longer be slaves to sin. (Rom. 6:6)

> Therefore, if anyone is in Christ, he is a new creation; the *old* has gone, the new has come! (2 Cor. 5:17)

> You were taught, with regard to your former way of life, to put off your *old* self, which is being corrupted by its deceitful desires. (Eph. 4:22)

> Do not lie to each other, since you have taken off your *old* self with its practices. (Col. 3:9)

"Old" is a choice. So is "New." We choose which one to receive and live by.

Nicodemus was "old." He admitted as much when he asked Christ, "How can a man be born when he is *old*?" (John 3:4). He had to have felt old. Nicodemus was a leader in the oldest religion in history. As a Pharisee, Nicodemus was the guardian, protector, and promoter of an old religion with old rules and old traditions. He wanted something new. He wanted to be new. So in his desperation he came to Jesus at night, risking his reputation and his position and searching for the secret of life.

So Jesus started at the beginning—birth.

It seems like a lot of births occur at night. All of the births in my family have begun at night. If it were up to my wife and me, labor would be short and sweet, beginning about 9:00 in the morning—after a good night's sleep—and ending with an easy delivery before lunch, freeing the afternoon up for a pleasant nap.

It never happened like that. Each of our children decided to begin the birth process in the middle of the night.

Nicodemus began his birth in the middle of the night, too.

Nicodemus saw something new in Jesus that could only come from God. He acknowledged, "No one could perform the miraculous signs you are doing if God were not with him" (John 3:2). Jesus replied by answering a question that Nicodemus didn't ask, but should have. Jesus said, "I tell you the truth, no one can see the kingdom of God unless he is born again" (John 3:3).

Nicodemus thought he was seeing the kingdom of God through his leadership as a Pharisee. He thought that he saw the kingdom of God in the rituals and traditions of his religion; however, he was seeing man's kingdom, not God's. Jesus told him that he could not see the kingdom of God unless he left the womb that he was dwelling in. He was living in a dark place. He was safe, but limited and trapped in a womb of his own design.

The womb is a dark place. Safe ... but dark. Comfortable ... but dark. Within the womb of his legalistic form of Judaism, Nicodemus could only—and would only—see shadows of the light of grace dancing just beyond his reality. Jesus wanted Nicodemus to leave the womb he was trapped in and find newness. Growth makes the womb obsolete, and if Nicodemus would allow Christ to deliver him, he would experience the type of dynamic growth God dreams of for all of his children.

I'm not sure—the Bible doesn't say—but I don't think Nicodemus was "old" for very much longer. In chapter 19 of the gospel of John, we find that Nicodemus took care of the body of Christ.

John noted:

> Later, Joseph of Arimathea asked Pilate for the body of
> Jesus. Now Joseph was a disciple of Jesus, but secretly
> because he feared the Jews. With Pilate's permission, he
> came and took the body away. He was accompanied by

Nicodemus, the man who earlier had visited Jesus at night. *Nicodemus* brought a mixture of myrrh and aloes, about seventy-five pounds. Taking Jesus' body, the two of them wrapped it, with the spices, in strips of linen. This was in accordance with Jewish burial customs. (John 19:38–40)

I hope that Nicodemus experienced spiritual birth. It's life changing and unforgettable.

Although I don't remember my physical birth, I *do* remember the birth of my spirit. I can still remember every detail. It was on an April morning, and I was—for the first time—keenly aware that I was not perfect. I was a sinner and I needed hope. I needed a second chance. I needed forgiveness.

I also knew that Jesus was who he said he was. I believed in him with all of my heart, and I wanted to be called by his name for the rest of eternity: "Christian—like Jesus."

I was spiritually born on Easter morning, 1978. My mother was there, my father was there, and my Savior was there ... delivering me.

When I rose up out of the water, I felt new. I felt reborn. I felt rejuvenated. I felt hopeful. I felt I had a purpose in life.

Legend has it that when he was depressed or when feelings of anguish would prowl around him, Martin Luther would recall the Latin words, *Baptizatus sum*. I have been baptized! He was proclaiming, "I am not old! I am new! And I have a purpose in life!"

Every meaningful thing I do today is because I was born again. My salvation gave me hope. My salvation gave me purpose. My salvation gave me an abundant life.

Have you been born again or are you old?

My wife and I just found out that we're having another child—our fourth—and it's a girl! We thought we were done, but God had another plan. I can't wait for our daughter to be born. I long to see her grow, dream, and live an abundant life.[1]

God feels the same way about you.

◪ REFUEL!

1. Go to the baby nursery in your house or church or to the baby section at a local department store and read John 3.

2. Answer this question—honestly, "Have you been born again?" If not, why not? You don't have to be old anymore. You can live a new life. The apostle Paul wrote this:

> What shall we say, then? Shall we go on sinning so that grace may increase? By no means! We died to sin; how can we live in it any longer? Or don't you know that all of us who were baptized into Christ Jesus were baptized into his death? We were therefore buried with him through baptism into death in order that, just as Christ was raised from the dead through the glory of the Father, we too may live a new life. (Rom. 6:1–4)

You can give your life to Christ today and be born again "of water and the spirit" (John 3:5).

3. Go to the store and purchase childbirth announcements or create one on your computer. Pick one out and write the date you were born of the spirit. Include all of the important details.

4. Keep the childbirth announcement where you can see it, remembering the day your life became new.

Worship

Whoever drinks the water I give him will never thirst. Indeed, the water I give him will become in him a spring of water welling up to eternal life.

—John 4:14

Have you ever been really thirsty? I mean desperately thirsty.

My son Sylas has been waking up angry and early. Recently, my wife and I have found ourselves awakened from a deep sleep several times each night by the screaming of our ten-month-old son. It's a *uniquely* pleasant experience.

One of us—my wife or I—will stumble to the kitchen, grab a bottle of milk from the refrigerator, nuke it in the microwave for forty seconds, shuffle to Sylas's room, pick up our "patient" son, sit down on the couch, give him the bottle, and listen to him gulp. After his thirst is satisfied, we place him back in his crib, and—within seconds—he's back to sleep while my wife and I spend the next couple of hours tirelessly trying to join him in the Land of Nod.

But Rhonda and I don't really mind this nightly ritual because we understand what it's like to be thirsty.

We all thirst. We're born thirsty—for more than we know. God created us to desire not only physical water, but spiritual water, too.

In his book *The "God" Part of the Brain*, Matthew Alper poses a mind-boggling premise. He suggests that our minds are "hard-wired" to believe in and worship God. He himself doesn't believe in God. He says that God is simply "a cluster of neurons from which spiritual cognitions, sensations, and behaviors are generated."[1]

Whereas Mr. Alper concludes that his research proves that God merely exists within us, I draw a different conclusion. I think his study confirms that God created us with a thirst: a thirst to worship him. We are wired that way. We have a holy craving to submit to, to follow, and to praise something or someone bigger than ourselves. If it's not God, then it will be something else.

That's why I act so crazy at Orlando Magic basketball games. I love sports. When I go to a Magic game, I act like a maniac. I cheer, clap, jump, dance, yell at the referees, and do the wave. There's something about sports that draws my attention and my affection. That kind of unbridled passion seems to come naturally—like I was made for it.

The same urge overwhelms me at a good movie, in the presence of the perfect pepperoni pizza, during the final lap of the Daytona 500 when Jeff Gordon trades paint with Dale Earnhardt Jr., and while watching the sunset over the Gulf of Mexico.

Last spring my family and I were visiting St. Petersburg Beach. We were ordering "health food" at Wendy's when the girl behind the register became our travel agent. She said, "Are you all from out of town?"

"Yes," I replied cautiously.

She then said, "Then you won't want to miss the sunset at the beach. It's amazing."

Convinced, we said, "Make our order to go."

When we arrived on the beach, we found a diverse crowd of about 100 strangers gathered for worship. Our church was the beach. Our pews were beach chairs and towels. Our worship leader was the sun.

The sky was clear of clouds and crowded with color as the

sea swallowed the golden sun. We—the strangers and I—watched in silence as God painted the sky with brilliant light and color. When it was over and darkness began to replace the light, the crowd in which I stood erupted in applause. I didn't start it, but I eagerly joined in as we spontaneously applauded the sunset. One hundred strangers witnessed something that happens every day and unanimously decided that the only appropriate response was applause. That was worship. That's what we were all designed to do.

We are wired for worship. We thirst for it, we crave it. The problem is we satisfy our thirst with the wrong things: sports, movies, TV, money, toys, and scrapbooking. None of these things are bad by themselves, but as a substitute for worshiping our Creator, they just don't satisfy. God made us thirsty for *him*. When we try to satisfy our thirst from the wells of this world, we remain thirsty. If we continue to drink what we should not be drinking, we will die.

I'm fascinated with the story of the USS *Indianapolis*, a naval battle cruiser. On July 30, 1945, the *Indianapolis*, after delivering key parts for the atom bomb that was dropped on Hiroshima, was torpedoed by a Japanese submarine in the South Pacific. Two weeks before the end of World War II, 1,200 men found themselves in a fight for their survival. An estimated 300 men were killed in the initial explosion, and the other 900 men were suddenly floating in the ocean. The Navy did not realize that the ship was missing right away, so the men were left for five long days to fight for their survival. Hypothermia, exhaustion, sharks, and dehydration took their toll on the survivors.

It's a story of courage. It's a story of endurance. It's a story of unhealthy thirst. It's also a story of heroes. One of those heroes was the ship's doctor, Dr. Lewis Haynes. Last summer I had the privilege of attending a reunion of the USS *Indianapolis* survivors at a hotel in downtown Indianapolis. At that reunion, one of the survivors told me through tearful eyes of how Dr. Haynes desperately worked to save the lives of the survivors as they floated in the ocean. He would swim among the 900 sailors trying to keep them alive by offering them both hope and warnings. One of his biggest battles was trying to keep them from drinking saltwater.

This was next to impossible because it didn't seem to make any sense. How do you convince thirsty men not to drink the water they are floating in? Yet he had to. He knew that drinking the saltwater would be certain death.

Ocean water contains seven times more salt than the human body can safely digest. When drinking it, a person dehydrates because the kidneys demand extra water to flush the overload of salt. The more saltwater someone drinks, the thirstier he gets and if he keeps on drinking, he will actually die of thirst. So Haynes swam to each man and begged him to deny his thirst.

The men who gave up and gave in to the temptation to drink ocean water died horrible deaths, some choking on their own swollen tongues and others slipping into comas and then drifting with foam-filled mouths down into the darkness of the sea.

When the nightmare was over and they were rescued, only 317 men were still alive. What if more of those men had resisted their unhealthy thirst? How many lives would have been saved?

Jesus encountered a thirsty woman at a well in Samaria. He swam into her world urging her not to drink the water she was floating in.

Jesus was in Judea and many people were becoming his disciples. This was agitating the Pharisees, so Jesus left Judea and entered Samaria, apparently to avoid a premature conflict with the jealous Jewish leaders. It wasn't time for that battle yet.

His trip took him north through Samaria and to a noon-time stop at Jacob's well in a town called Sychar. He was tired. He wanted to rest and give a drink of water. Yes—*give* a drink of water. He was the personification of water, and he was about to offer himself to a thirsty outcast.

While he was resting, a Samaritan woman came to get some water, so Jesus spoke to her and broke almost every unspoken social rule that existed in his day. He—a Jewish man—spoke to a Samaritan woman. Jews didn't do this. They avoided "contamination." Samaritans were disliked by their neighbors because they were considered to have impure blood lines. In 721 BC, Samaria was invaded and destroyed by Sargon of Assyria. He carried all but a remnant of the Samaritans away to captivity. The remnant that remained intermarried with the Assyrians, creating a mixed race—a race of people hated by the Jews because they were considered unclean.

Adding to the prejudice was an incident that occurred at Passover several years after the birth of Christ. During Passover, the gates of the Temple would open at midnight. Sometime around the years AD 6–9, some Samaritan hoodlums intruded the Temple and polluted the Holy Place with human bones. This violation led to Samaritans being excluded from religious services and increased prejudice against them. Their food, their life, and their presence were all considered unclean.

So, Jesus didn't have to talk to this woman. In fact, he really shouldn't have talked to her for another big reason: she was a woman. At this time in history, Jewish men didn't talk to women in public. But Jesus *did* talk to this woman because he wanted to teach her—and us—how to satisfy our spiritual thirst.

This woman had been to the well of pleasure. She had been married five times and was now living with a man who was not her husband. But she was still thirsty.

She'd been to the well of organized religion. She understood the debate between the Samaritans and Jews over the true place of worship (see John 4:19–20). She even knew that the Messiah was coming (see John 4:25). But she was still thirsty.

What was her problem?

Her problem is often our problem: we long for more than this well offers. We go to the well of pleasure for a drink, but leave thirsty. We go to the well of organized religion, but leave thirsty. We must learn the lesson this Samaritan woman learned: the only way to truly satisfy the thirsting of our soul is to worship God. We must not drink the water we are floating in.

This world is full of deadly pleasures that promise to satisfy but only leave us feeling empty. Worship of God, however, is healing and satisfying and can fill our deepest needs. That is one of the reasons I'm so disheartened by Christians who allow themselves to be divided by worship styles.

 ## REFUEL!

1. Get a glass of water from the sink or a water fountain and drink it while you read John 4.

2. While reflecting on John 4, take a small piece of paper and list the top three things you thirst for in this world.

3. Tear up the paper into small pieces and dump it into your glass of water.

4. While holding your now polluted glass of water, ask yourself this question: "Am I still thirsty?"

5. Pray, asking God to fill you with a thirst for the "Living Water."

6. Get a fresh glass of water. Drink up.

I received a phone call the other night from a friend in Indiana. Her church is divided over worship. The young people are desperate to sing some choruses. The older people refuse to sing anything that's not in the hymnbook, so they sit with crossed arms and closed lips during each chorus. I wanted to tell my friend: "There is nothing new under the sun" (Eccl. 1:9).

Worship has always been a controversial issue. Worship is controversial because it's all about God and, at the same time, all about man. Worship without God will never satisfy us. Worship without man will never satisfy God. God wants everything from us, and we want everything for ourselves. Therein lies the tension that gives birth to the controversy.

Now, we magnify the controversy by trivializing *worship* by using the word to only describe the time of music and singing within our worship services. It may surprise that there is nothing in the encounter between Jesus and the Samaritan woman at Jacob's well that involves music.

That's because worship is so much more than singing and playing music to God.

We worship when we live a life that praises God and gives glory to his name. We worship when we serve others in a way that honors God. We worship when we give his gifts back to him to thank him for all that he's given us. We worship when we read his Word and praise him for giving it to us. And we worship when we gather in his name and sing to him.

Through the encounter at the well, we learn two reasons why we need to worship. First, worship satisfies our thirst for the spiritual. "God is spirit" (John 4:24), and since we are made in his image, we are spiritual beings, too. We were, therefore, made to worship God spiritually. Worship is a struggle between the physical and the spiritual because we like things we can see, touch, and hear; but worship is solely a spiritual event.

The second lesson Jesus taught the Samaritan woman is that worshiping God satisfies our thirst for truth. He told her, "Yet a time is coming and has now come when the true worshipers will worship the Father in spirit and truth" (John 4:23).

Have you ever been lied to? "I never forward e-mails like

this, but there is a little boy in England who is dying and is trying to collect cards from around the world...." "The check's in the mail." "I'm from the government and I'm here to help you." "You don't look fat." "I promise I'll stop drinking." "I'd never cheat on you." "I do."

It's no fun to be lied to.

This woman had been lied to. She'd been lied to by the men she'd married. She'd also been lied to by the men who were her religious leaders. The Samaritan Bible contained only the Pentateuch (the first five books of the Old Testament). She had only been given a portion of God's story. They worshiped the true God, but their failure to accept the truth of the revelations about the Messiah meant they missed all of the important prophecies about Jesus. The Samaritans "worship what [they] do not know; we worship what we do know" (John 4:22).

But Jesus told her four important truths:

The first was that God is real. There is a God who is standing here before you offering you "living water" (John 4:10). God is real and that certainty is one of the reasons we worship him in spite of not seeing him.

Another was that God knows us—intimately. Jesus, God incarnate, already knew that the woman at the well was living with a man who wasn't her husband. The Truth said, "You are right when you say you have no husband. The fact [truth] is, you have had five husbands, and the man you now have is not your husband. What you have just said is quite true" (John 4:17–18).

The next truth was that God wants us to know him. Jesus continued, "You Samaritans worship what you do not know; we worship what we do know" (John 4:22). The Samaritans were missing the Messiah. They didn't know him. God wants us to know him and when we worship we give ourselves an opportunity to know him more.

In John 4:23–24, Jesus told this woman a final and most

amazing truth: God wants us to worship him. Jesus said, "Yet a time is coming and has now come when the true worshipers will worship the Father in spirit and truth, for they are the kind of worshipers the Father *seeks*. God is spirit, and his worshipers must worship in spirit and truth."

One phrase always jumps out at me: "for they are the kind of worshipers the Father seeks." The word used here for "seek" is the Greek word *zeteo*, which is only used nine times in the New Testament. This word means, "to crave." Amazing! God craves our worship.

Any parent of a child understands this "craving." It's what we feel as the words "I love you" flow for the first time from the lips of the children we have cherished since before their birth. God craves our love. Let's give it to him.

This event closes with five enlightening words. In passing, John wrote, "Then, leaving her water jar ..." (John 4:28). What? She was thirsty. She came to the well with a water jar because she was physically thirsty. But when she left, she left her water jar. That doesn't make any sense to people who drink only the water of this world, but it makes perfect sense to anyone who, like this woman, has enjoyed the first sip of living water. She left her jar because she didn't care about her physical thirst anymore. All she wanted was to satisfy her thirst for the spiritual and the truthful.

Are you thirsty? Don't drink the water you're floating in. It will kill you. Come to Jesus each day and let him satisfy your spiritual thirst. If you do, you'll set down your water jar and never be thirsty again.

GROWTH

At once the man was cured; he picked up his mat and walked.

—*John 5:9*

Change is not always bad.
Change is not always good.
But change *is* a part of life.

We see change in our bodies: feet get bigger, legs get longer, hips expand, hair falls out from where it's supposed to be and appears where it shouldn't be.

We see change in nature: summer becomes fall; fall becomes winter; winter becomes spring; and spring becomes summer again. God never changes, but he has woven change into the natural world for our sake. The changing of seasons restores all of God's creation.

We see rapid change in technology: It took forty years for radio to reach fifty million users and fourteen years for TV to reach fifty million users, but only four years for the Internet to reach fifty million users. A weekday edition of the New York *Times* carries more information than the average person in the seventeenth century would digest in a lifetime, and my watch contains more computing power than existed in the entire world before 1961.

It has been estimated that more information has been generated in the last thirty years than in the previous five thousand.

Leonard Sweet, in his book *Soul Tsunami* observed, "We are now living in a world where it is cheaper, faster, and safer to send a signal over twenty thousand miles up to a satellite and back again than it is to walk the fifty feet to tell you that your child is crying or your table is ready."[1]

This world is full of change. Leonard Sweet also reminded us that in the 1950s, movies were seventy-five cents, a new Chevy was $1,220, a year at Harvard was $525, a first-class stamp was three cents, and the most basic computer was $500,000. At that time, most businesses were closed on Sundays, a school's biggest problem was chewing gum, and a "crack salesman" meant that he was really good at what he did. It also used to be that you worked with one company until you retired. What used to be is no longer. Change happens.

The world is constantly changing around us. Sometimes I feel like Sergei Krikalev. Sergei Krikalev isn't a household name; I found out about him in a story posted by Denver Seminary on the Internet. In April 1991, he was living a comfortable life in Leningrad. He believed in the Communist Party, endorsed the leadership of Mikhail Gorbachev, and dismissed Boris Yeltsin as a political nobody.

Krikalev was a part of the Soviet space program and was launched into space on an extended mission. However, his four-month mission turned into a ten-month mission when he couldn't return to earth because the Soviet Union had torn apart at the seams. By the time Krikalev finally landed on the earth, what had been the former USSR had become the Commonwealth of Independent States. His hometown of Leningrad had been renamed St. Petersburg, Gorbachev had turned into a capitalist and was signing million-dollar book deals, and the insignificant Yeltsin was President of Russia.

In less than a year, without warning, and while Krikalev circled the earth, a new era had begun. Krikalev's life changed dramatically while he was in space. Think about that. When I read about this story for the first time, I wondered what Sergei was thinking while he orbited the globe. How much did he know about the changes that were occurring. I wondered if he ever thought, *Wow, will they get me back down from here? The whole country is disintegrating and the folks who are supposed to know how to get me down don't work there anymore.* Wouldn't that be a trip? Change came to Sergei. Change comes to us, too.

Change is a part of life.

In fact, change *is* life.

◹ REFUEL!

1. Rent and watch the movie Big, *in which Tom Hanks plays a boy whose world—and body—are changed over night.*

2. What lessons can we learn from this movie about dealing with change?

Skin replaces itself every month, the stomach lining every five days, the liver every six weeks, the skeleton every three months, and the cheek cells three times a day. Ninety-eight percent of the atoms in our bodies are replaced every year. Our whole bodies change every five (men) to seven (women) years.

Our kids change so quickly. My youngest son is on the verge of walking, and my wife and I are encouraging this important event. It would be unthinkable to discourage the process. We hold him up and cheer each little step toward independence. The pride and joy of carrying my son in my arms would turn to heartbreak and shame if I'm still carrying him around when he's thirty.

We want—and expect—our children to grow, walk, and experience all that God has planned for their lives.

That's why, as recorded in John 5, Jesus told a paralytic man to walk. While in Jerusalem, Jesus saw a man who had been unable to walk for almost four decades. Jesus found him sitting by a pool of water called Bethesda. In the time of Christ, people would gather around this particular pool because it had a strange flow caused by the spring that was its source. If you'll notice in your Bible, one verse from this account has been left out of most modern translations. In the omitted verse (John 5:4, which can be found in the notes section of most translations), we read that the people believed a supernatural force caused the irregular flow of the pool, and the first person to enter the rippling water would be healed. This pool was more than water; it was hope that welled up and immersed the broken.

The hope found in those waters, though diluted with ancient and mystical tales of visiting angels, still beckoned those desperate for healing. This seemed the paralytic's only chance for recovery. If he could dip in the pool when the water stirred, his life would be changed. But every time the water moved, he sat helplessly watching others take their turn splashing in the hope.

This pool was the paralytic's only hope … until his only Hope saw him. Jesus saw people; he really looked at them. He didn't walk by them acting as if he were more interested in his feet, his newspaper, or his latest cell phone call. He looked at the very people that we often pretend we don't see.

On this day, Jesus saw a man who needed a change. John's account reveals that Jesus "learned that he had been in this condition for a long time" (John 5:6). It was time for a change, which could only begin with a timeless question we all must answer: "Do you want to get well?" (John 5:6).

The invalid was essentially being asked if he was content with watching the world walk by when he was destined to join in the stroll. Did he like sitting where he was sitting, or was he willing to do what it took to grow?

We all must answer Jesus' question as well.

I had a mat one time. It was red on one side, blue on the other, and my name was printed on one corner in black marker ink. I loved that mat. I slept on it every day. I was comfortable on it. Periodically, I woke up with a puddle of drool beside my face on my mat. It was a great mat.

I don't have that mat anymore. There was a time when it became inappropriate for me to have it. That day was the first day of first grade. My faithful red and blue mat had seen me through nap time every day at kindergarten, but I didn't need it any longer. So, I folded it up and put it in my closet.

There comes a point in our lives when we have to pick up our mat and walk. The invalid was at such a point.

Jesus asked him if he wanted to get well and the only answer the invalid could give was an excuse. Excuses are worthless. If "ifs" and "buts" were candies and nuts, we'd all have a wonderful Christmas.

Excuse 1: "I have no one to help me" (John 5:7).

We must independently decide to grow. There may be no one to help you, but we all have a choice and we can decide to help ourselves. You may feel alone in your pain and have understandable reasons to feel that way. You may actually be alone, but you must be confident that God wants to help you by empowering you to help yourself.

Excuse 2: "While I am trying to get in, someone else goes down ahead of me" (John 5:7).

We must take the initiative to position ourselves for growth. Our condition is not always someone else's fault. Sometimes, we blame others for things that are our responsibility. There may be many who seem like they want to keep you from the healing that God has predestined for you, but it's up to you to do what it takes to grow.

Jesus' response to the paralytic's excuses was "Get up! Pick up your mat and walk" (John 5:8).

Jesus' response to our excuses is still "Get up! Pick up your mat and walk."

"At once the man ..." Did you notice that this is the first time in the text that this paralyzed person is referred to as a "man"? Up to this point he had been referred to as "the paralyzed," "one," and "the invalid," but John now testifies that he is a man.

"At once the man was cured; he picked up his mat and walked." Christ wants us to grow. Every healthy thing grows.

An interesting event happened shortly after the healing. John recorded, "Later Jesus found him at the temple ..." (John 5:14). Did you catch that? That was a sign of growth. This man was no longer worshiping bubbles in a pool of well water; he was now at the temple worshiping the Creator of that water. Worshiping God instead of wallowing in self-pity is a sign of spiritual growth.

Returning to the text, John wrote, "Later Jesus found him at the temple and said to him, 'See, you are well again. Stop sinning or something worse may happen to you'" (John 5:14).

Arron's translation reads, "Keep growing or you'll find yourself sitting back at the pool of Bethesda with the other broken and hurting people."

My friends, God loves you and wants you to grow. Pick up your mat and walk.

RETREAT

Jesus, knowing that they intended to come and make him king by force,
withdrew again to a mountain by himself.

—*John 6:15*

R etreat is not typically viewed as a good thing. The motto of the French Foreign Legion is, "If I falter, push me on. If I stumble, pick me up. If I retreat, shoot me." There aren't too many movies that celebrate armies who retreat. In the first twenty minutes of the movie *Saving Private Ryan*, I was overcome with tears as I watched those men leave the safety of their boats and advance on the beach at Normandy, undaunted by the German tsunami of bullets, fire, and fear. The heroes of D-Day were heroes not because they retreated, but because they advanced. In war, retreat is almost always the first sign of imminent defeat ... but not always.

Remember MacArthur?

Douglas MacArthur loved the Philippines. He initially visited the islands during his first assignment out of West Point as a lieutenant with an engineer corps. He was sent back to the Philippines with his wife in 1925, but the New York heiress was not happy on the island MacArthur loved so much. He *retreated* to the States to try to salvage his marriage, but three years later, the marriage finally ended.

MacArthur then *retreated* to the Philippines, where he commanded the Army's Philippine Department until he again returned to the States to be the Army's Chief of Staff in 1930. This assignment, in the midst of the Great Depression, was heart-breakingly difficult. He suffered in this post for five years before once again *retreating* to the Philippines to head a U.S. military mission charged with preparing the islands for full independence in 1946. The next few years were among the happiest in MacArthur's life. On his way to Manila, he met and fell in love with thirty-seven-year-old Jean Marie Faircloth from Murfreesboro, Tennessee. They had a son and enjoyed their lives in Manila until a threat from the expansionist Japanese empire became too great to ignore.

MacArthur began preparing a resistance force in the Philippines to resist the Japanese. After the Japanese attack at Pearl Harbor on December 7, 1941, MacArthur knew the island nation was doomed. Within a month, the Japanese had destroyed his air force, ravaged his army, and the American troops had retreated to the Bataan peninsula, where they struggled to survive. With heartbreak and anger, MacArthur watched the Philippines fall into the hands of the Japanese.

Back in the States, President Roosevelt was concerned for more than just the Philippines. He was concerned for the reputation of America's most famous general, so he ordered MacArthur to withdraw to Australia. MacArthur didn't want to leave, but he did. He retreated, but defiantly promised as he departed from the place he so dearly loved, "I shall return." And for three years, the world watched as MacArthur diligently fought to keep his promise. Then in October of 1944, the world watched as he dramatically waded ashore at Leyte, and in the following months, liberated the rest of the Philippines. Sometimes it's good to retreat.

MacArthur's retreat ultimately guaranteed victory and new life for the people of the Philippines.

We don't seem to understand the value of retreat in our lives. We push ahead as if we are invincible and act resentful of anything that slows down our pursuit of what we think we need for a more abundant life. And this resentment of retreat begins early.

I hated to take a nap when I was five. I would pretend I was asleep when I was really awake. Now I act like I'm awake when I'm really asleep. Sometimes I wish somebody would send me to bed.

As children, we hate to stop. I can't tell you how many times throughout my childhood I heard, "Stop running in the halls!" "Stop running in the house!" "Stop running in the church!" I eventually did, but I didn't like it. I hated to stop; I had places to go.

As adults, we still hate to stop. We have places to go and we want to get there fast. In fact, we want to do everything fast.

We eat fast.

In his book *The Life You've Always Wanted*, John Ortberg observes, "We worship at the shrine of the Golden Arches, not because they sell 'good food,' or even 'cheap food,' but because it is 'fast food.' Even after fast food was introduced, people still had to park their cars, go inside, order, and take their food to a table, all of which took time. So we invented the Drive-Thru Lane to enable families to eat in vans, as nature intended."[1]

We also drive fast.

Recently, I heard about a guy riding in a taxi in a metropolitan area. Coming to a red light, the taxi driver sailed right on through. The passenger said, "Hey watch it! That light was red."

The cabbie replied, "Don't worry, my brother does it all the time."

The next light was red, and the cabbie barreled right on through. The man yelled, "Hey pal, you're going to get me killed!"

"Oh, don't worry about it; my brother does it all the time."

The next light was green. The driver slammed on his brakes. Confused and irritated, the passenger cried, "What's your problem, the light is green?"

"Yeah, but you never know when my brother might be coming through."

Hurrying has consequences. Living in the fast lane only means that we get to the toll booth quicker.

For too many of us, life has become a race for what we think we want only to find that the prize we thought we wanted wasn't really worth wanting in the first place.

My family and I moved to Florida when I was eight. In Florida, we were exposed to many new and exciting things that we didn't have in Hamilton, Ohio: tacky T-shirt shops, orange trees, alligators, tourists, and dog tracks. One of my first memories of Florida is of my first and last visit to a dog track. My dad was the guest speaker at a church in South Florida, and the member we were staying with happened to own a dog track. Our host thought it would be a good idea to take a preacher and his family to a place where people drink, gamble, and yell at dogs. Good idea. Well, we went. My parents had never heard of a dog track and, after quickly assessing the situation, concluded that we shouldn't be there. My sisters, brother, and I sensed that we were tasting forbidden fruit, so the events of that night became larger than life. I remember standing trackside watching those beautiful dogs rip around a brightly lit dirt track with crowds cheering their effort. The sights and sounds were unforgettable: the crescendo of the crowd as the dogs neared the finish line, the sounds of the dogs' feet pounding the neatly groomed dirt, and the high-pitched squeal of the plastic rabbit circling the track just beyond the reach of the dogs. It may have been sinful ... but it was exciting.

I watched race after race in amazement as those graceful dogs chased that plastic rabbit. That's why I was so shocked to see what happened in the fifth race of the evening. Halfway around the second turn and right before my strategic position on the back stretch, the rabbit stopped. Now this was going to be exciting! My eight-year-old young male heart could not wait to see these dogs devour the plastic rabbit they had been so desperately pursuing.

But nothing happened.

The rabbit stopped. Then, the dogs stopped and sat down in their places. It was bizarre. Not one dog made an attempt to sniff the rabbit—or even sneak a lick. They acted like the rabbit didn't exist anymore. They just sat down in the dirt acting uninterested. I don't know why I was surprised. It was a plastic rabbit, and dogs don't normally eat plastic rabbits. But that left me wondering, *Why were they chasing a rabbit they didn't really want to catch?*

Sometimes we are like those dogs: chasing plastic rabbits only to find that once the rabbit is attainable, it isn't something that ever will satisfy. We chase promotions—only to taste the bitterness of stress. We chase possessions—only to taste the bitterness of overwhelming debt. We chase illicit sex—only to taste the bitterness of guilt. We chase our selfish desires—only to taste the bitterness of loneliness.

Yet, we still long for the rabbit. It is just out of reach so we convince ourselves that we must get to the office an hour earlier each day or stay a few hours longer. We are so close to the rabbit—we must take one more call. We must get just one more thing done. We must check our e-mail one more time. We must finish just one more project. We must not stop or we might lose our place in the rat race. This is all wrong.

The only thing we need to do is the very thing we often refuse to do—stop. We must stop! May I get preachy here? Who do we think we are—God? Because, if we *were* God we'd know the importance of stopping and retreating into rest.

God stopped. "By the seventh day God had finished the work he had been doing; so on the seventh day he rested from all his work" (Gen. 2:2).

(Excuse me. It's 11:44 p.m. and I'm struck by the hypocrisy revealed in the difference between what I'm writing and what I'm living. Twenty minutes ago my wife said, "Good night honey, I'm going to bed." And here I sit … like an idiot … typing words telling about the importance of "stopping" … and denying my own need to stop. So, I'm going to put my money where my mouth is and my body next to where my wife is. I'm tired, so I think I'll retreat to my bedroom for now.)

I'm back, and I'm ready to go again. It's amazing how good it feels to retreat.

We need to follow the example of Christ.

In his ministry here on earth, Jesus retreated often. In John 6, we find great crowds of people following him because he was doing miraculous work and healing many sick people. At some point as Jesus sat with his disciples beside the Sea of Galilee watching a great crowd of people gather, he decided to do something cool.

He tested Philip—the disciple who had such a heart for people that he would one day have "the evangelist" added to his name— by asking him, "Where shall we buy bread for these people to eat?" (John 6:5). Jesus already knew what he was going to do.

Philip answered this rhetorical question with the obvious answer, "It's impossible!"

Suddenly, a boy with five pieces of bread and a couple of fish appeared on the scene. I don't know whether Andrew found him or if he found Andrew, but this boy's meager meal was their only option.

Jesus went to work. He blessed the food and turned a sack lunch into twelve baskets full of leftovers. The people he fed were amazed and ready to give him a promotion. He would be on the fast track to financial independence and better able to provide for his followers. He would be important. He would be advancing his position. He would have to work more hours and sacrifice more, but … he would be king.

Jesus knew that the people were trying to force their will upon him, and he wasn't going to allow it to happen. They had *tasted* his power and were ready for Christ to unleash that power on their enemies as their king. They determined that he needed to advance. Jesus knew how to say no. He needed to retreat. "Jesus withdrew again." Did you catch what John wrote? Jesus retreated, "again." Retreating was a common thing for Christ to do. Consider the following examples:

> When Jesus heard what had happened, he withdrew by boat privately to a solitary place. Hearing of this, the crowds followed him on foot from the towns.
> —Matthew 14:13

> After he had dismissed them, he went up on a mountainside by himself to pray. When evening came, he was there alone.
> —Matthew 14:23

> Leaving that place, Jesus withdrew to the region of Tyre and Sidon.
> —Matthew 15:21

> Very early in the morning, while it was still dark, Jesus got up, left the house and went off to a solitary place, where he prayed.
> —Mark 1:35

> Jesus withdrew with his disciples to the lake, and a large crowd from Galilee followed.
> —Mark 3:7

> But Jesus often withdrew to lonely places and prayed.
> —Luke 5:16

> He withdrew about a stone's throw beyond them, knelt down and prayed.
> —Luke 22:41

To guarantee victory for himself and life for us, Jesus retreated. His most famous retreat is actually promised in John 14 as he tried to comfort his closest friends with two important promises:

> "Do not let your hearts be troubled. Trust in God; trust also in me. In my Father's house are many rooms; if it were not so, I would have told you. *I am going there to prepare a place for you.* And if I go and prepare a place for you, *I will come back* and take you to be with me that you also may be where I am." (John 14:1–3)

Jesus promised two important things. First, he promised to retreat: "I am going." Second, he promised to return: "I will come back." He was saying to his disciples then and now, "I shall return!"

Christ's retreat ultimately guaranteed victory and new life for us.

The life and example of Jesus clears up the four most common misconceptions about retreat:

LIE: RETREAT IS AN ACT OF FEAR.
TRUTH: RETREAT IS AN ACT OF FAITH.

Sometimes, it takes more courage to walk away. Jesus, unlike many of his followers, was not a slave to fear. He was and is the master of faith. His many retreats were proof that Christ trusted that his Father's plan was better and that his Father's timing was perfect. Christ retreated because he had faith in his Father.

I challenge you to step out in faith, even if that means stepping back. Remember, retreating in fear breaks the spirit; retreating in faith emboldens the soul.

LIE: RETREAT IS A SIGN OF WEAKNESS.
TRUTH: RETREAT IS A SIGN OF STRENGTH.

Weak armies retreat to avoid pending defeat, but strong Christians retreat knowing victory is imminent. In John 6, we see a strong Jesus retreating to avoid a premature victory. It took strength for Christ to stand up to the mobs who couldn't wait for him to be king. It also took strength to submit to his Father's will rather than his own desires.

I challenge you to demonstrate true strength by retreating from untimely battles that may ultimately keep you from the victory that will come when the timing is right.

LIE: RETREAT IS GOING BACKWARD.
TRUTH: RETREAT IS GOING FORWARD.

It's all a matter of perspective. Your coworkers, friends, and possibly even your family may think that your retreat into a closer fellowship with God is backward. They may insult you with comments like, "You can't be serious about this church thing," "Don't go and get all holy and righteous on us," or "You're not as fun since you've become a religious fanatic." But you must do what is necessary to maintain your relationship with your Lord.

I challenge you follow your holy passion for God and keep moving forward even if it means being accused of going the wrong way.

LIE: RETREAT IS AN ACT OF SOLITUDE.
TRUTH: RETREAT IS AN ACT OF INTIMACY.

This is one of the biggest misconceptions about retreat. Retreat is not an act of solitude. Christ did not retreat to be by himself, he retreated to be with his Father. We also do not retreat to be alone, but to be with God. It's a paradox, but it seems even more paradoxical that we can be alone with God in a room packed with people. And as we learned in chapter 4, God craves intimate attention from us.

I challenge you to leave the mass of noise and people often. Retreat—not to spend time alone, but to spend time with the One who loves you so much that he would sacrifice his life for yours.

It's not un-Christian to admit that we are tired.

It's not un-Christian to admit that we feel weak.

It's not un-Christian to admit that we feel overwhelmed with life.

It's not un-Christian for us to say "no" to the urgent in order to say "yes" to the significant.

It's not un-Christian to admit that we aren't God!

In fact, we are most like Christ when we retreat to be closer to God.

I think it's time to retreat.

REFUEL!

1. Find a book of matches. Not a box—the kind with a flap that folds over the matches.

2. Find a small piece of paper. On the piece of paper, list the top five activities you do each week (work, watch TV, sleep, etc.).

3. Open the book of matches, and on the inside cover, list the five activities you would do if you were going to die next Saturday night.

4. Compare the lists.

5. Go to a safe place—maybe in the bathroom over the toilet.

6. Pull one match out of the matchbook, strike it, and light the piece of paper. Now would be a good time to drop the burning paper into the toilet.

7. Read the list inside the matchbook out loud and then put the matchbook in your pocket.

8. Keep it close at all times and pull it out to read it whenever your life catches fire again.

Discernment

After this, Jesus went around in Galilee, purposely staying away from Judea
because the Jews there were waiting to take his life.

—John 7:1

Timing is important to success in so many areas of life.
Timing is important in humor. Recently, I tried to explain
to my four-year-old son, Levi, why his favorite knock-knock joke
(which he wrote himself)—"Knock, knock. Who's there? Pizza.
Pizza who? Wanna pizza me?"—is not as funny to his eleven-
year-old sister when she's in the middle of a slumber party with
her friends.

Timing is important in fishing. Sometimes the fish are biting
and sometimes they aren't, but if you want to catch Blue Fish off
the eastern coast of Florida, you have to know that the only time
they'll be there is when they are chasing finger mullet between
December and February.

Timing is important in business. The goal is to build the
lemonade stand on Wall Street before New York City grows up
around it. Internet businesses like eBay, Amazon, and Google
could not have existed just twenty years ago, but came along at
just the right time and are now Fortune 500 companies.

Timing is important in marriage. Trust me, it's not a good idea
to expect romantic feelings to flow from your wife toward you if
you spent the last hour watching *SportsCenter* on ESPN while she
spent the same period of time bathing the kids, folding the laundry,

picking up toys, packing lunches, feeding the fish, cleaning the kitchen, helping the kids find and put on their pajamas, making sure that they brushed their teeth, and tucking them into bed.

Yes, good timing is an important key to the success of so many things in life, but sometimes in life our timing is just a little off.

Sometimes, We Are in the Wrong Place at the Wrong Time.

You're behind the school bus when you're already late for work.

You make an emergency trip to the local convenience store to pick up a package of diapers only to encounter a line that stretches out the door of people buying lottery tickets for that night's drawing.

You're in the "10 items or fewer Cash Only" lane at the grocery store behind someone with 54 items who can't seem to find her credit card.

Sometimes, We Are in the Right Place at the Wrong Time.

You arrive at the bank ready to make a much-needed deposit only to find it's closed for Columbus Day.

You meet some friends at your favorite restaurant for lunch only to discover that the health inspectors beat you there and closed it down.

You finally get home from work—by way of the gym—and find that your son is already in bed, you missed hearing about the problem he had in class today with a bully, you missed helping him learn how to write a cursive *z*, and you missed kissing him on the forehead moments before he drifted off to sleep.

Sometimes, We Are in the Wrong Place at the Right Time.

The time is right to be home with your family, but you're in the wrong place returning e-mails to strangers.

The time is right to be wrestling with your kids on the living room floor, but you're in the wrong place fighting for a business deal to please a boss who plans on letting you go.

The time is right to be talking with your spouse about a problem in your marriage, but you're in the wrong place talking to a friend about your spouse.

The time is right to be sitting with your family in church, but you're more interested in walking around a golf course and hitting a little white ball into a plastic cup.

So much of our lives can be spent far away from where our true life is. Where we are is often not where we should be.

Yes—I said, "should be." Pack your bags; we're going on a guilt trip.

"Should be" is the place we feel guilty about not being.

We make one last phone call before leaving when we should be at home eating pork chops and applesauce with our family. We go to work early when we should be leaning over our kids' beds saying, "It's time to get up." We turn the TV on when we should be talking to our family about important things. We sit at the computer pointlessly surfing the web, or answering one more e-mail when we should be chatting with our neighbors about their vacation, how to kill chinch bugs in St. Augustine grass, how the weather changes every fifteen minutes, or what it takes to keep a marriage from falling apart.

My Grandpa Maxey was a wise man. His life was both humble and significant. He was a brilliant man but never advertised his credentials. Grandpa was just smart and said a lot of things that are now a permanent part of my family's lexicon. He was better than smart—he was wise.

One of the phrases he said that I still say today is, "You gotta' be where the bein' is."

(It might help you if you say this phrase with a bit of a country accent.)

"Bein' where the bein' is" is one of the key elements of an abundant life. It's being at the right place at the right time. That takes discernment.

Time is so valuable, yet we spend so much of it not "bein' where the bein' is." According to the *U.S. News and World Report,* in a lifetime, the average American will spend:[1]

- Six months sitting at stoplights.
- Eight months opening junk mail.
- Five years waiting in line.

Jesus had discernment. He knew the importance of bein' where the bein' is. In John 7 we see that Jesus clearly knew that at that moment, the bein' was in Galilee. There were people waiting to kill him in Judea, so he was in Galilee. Life was in Galilee; death was in Judea.

 REFUEL!

1. Listen to the song "Cat's in the Cradle" by Harry Chapin on the album by the same name.

2. What is the overall message of this song? Can you relate?

3. Are you where you should be?

4. What are you going to do today to "be where the bein' is"?

The brothers of Christ were not very discerning. His brothers wanted him to be at the wrong place at the wrong time. When his brothers saw that Jesus was staying away from Judea and was possibly missing a great opportunity to "make it big," they said, "You ought to leave here and go to Judea, so that your disciples may see the miracles you do. No one who wants to become a public figure acts in secret" (John 7:3–4). To this Jesus replied, "The *right time* for me has not yet come," and then added a little rebuke to his brothers by observing, "for you any time is right" (John 7:6).

That's me. Any time is the right time to me. I'm not a good wait-er. If I decide I want something, I want it now. No wonder I often feel like life is impacting me more than I'm impacting life. When we do something because we feel like the timing is right and neglect to consult the One who created all time, then we are foolish. Instead, we should ask God to help us discern when the time is right.

I want to be like Jesus. He had such godly discernment. He knew—more than his brothers—that it was not exactly the right time to be going to Judea. It was the right place but the wrong time. Christ's goal was not fame, but impact. He would go to Judea, but not until it was the right place at the right time. Jesus said to his undiscerning brothers, "You go to the Feast. I am *not yet* going up to this Feast, because for me the *right time* has not yet come" (John 7:8).

Jesus was definitely going to the Feast of Tabernacles, one of the three great feasts on the Jewish calendar during which every Jewish male was required by law to go to Jerusalem, but he wouldn't make his appearance until "halfway through the Feast" (John 7:14). That would be the right time for him to make the biggest impact.

Discernment is essential if we want to make an impact.

The Jews in Judea were not very discerning and they did not listen carefully. Jesus told the people that he and his teaching were from God: "My teaching is not my own. It comes from him who sent me" (John 7:16), but they concluded that Jesus was "demon-possessed" (John 7:20). They were not looking carefully. They watched Jesus heal a man who had been paralyzed for thirty-eight years (see John 5:2–9), but all they saw was a man who "broke" the Law of Moses by working on the Sabbath. They were so concerned with the fact that he was healing on the Sabbath that they were apathetic about the healing. Jesus rebuked them for "judging by mere appearances" and urged them to "make a right judgment" (John 7:24).

The "right judgment" for these people would have been that Jesus was the promised Messiah. He was the Son of God ... but they missed it ... they missed him, because they weren't very discerning, and for that reason, they missed being personally blessed by God.

The people were amazed at what they heard Jesus say and by what they saw him do, so they began to wonder aloud, "Have the authorities really concluded that he is the Christ? But we know where this man is from; when the Christ comes, no one will know where he is from" (John 7:26–27). Later they continued to be dismayed, "When the Christ comes, will he do more miraculous signs than this man?" (John 7:31).

Did you notice that?

"*When* he comes...."

He had come and was standing before them, but they were so undiscerning that they missed him.

Notice one other thing: within seven verses Jesus said "I am" five times.

> "But we know where this man is from; when the Christ comes, no one will know where he is from."
>
> Then Jesus, still teaching in the temple courts, cried out, "Yes, you know me, and you know where *I am* from. *I am* not here on my own, but he who sent me is true. You do not know him, but I know him because *I am* from him and he sent me."
>
> At this they tried to seize him, but no one laid a hand on him, because his time had not yet come. Still, many in the crowd put their faith in him. They said, "When the Christ comes, will he do more miraculous signs than this man?"
>
> The Pharisees heard the crowd whispering such things about him. Then the chief priests and the Pharisees sent temple guards to arrest him.
>
> Jesus said, "*I am* with you for only a short time, and

then I go to the one who sent me. You will look for me,
but you will not find me; and where *I am*, you cannot
come." (John 7:27–34)

Sound familiar?

When Moses was called to lead the Israelites out of Egyptian
bondage, he was worried about what he should say to convince
the Israelites that he was really sent by God. He essentially asked
God, "Who should I say has sent me?" To this God replied, "I AM
who I AM. This is what you are to say to the Israelites: 'I AM has
sent me to you'" (Exod. 3:14). I AM is God's name. I AM is Christ's
name, too.

In John 8, we find the Jewish people still not getting it. They
still think he's demon-possessed (see John 8:48), so Jesus tells
them his name in a way that even the undiscerning can't miss, "I
tell you the truth," Jesus answered, "before Abraham was born,
I am!" (John 8:58).

Jesus is telling them that the "I am" is here.

John 7:40 recounts a breakthrough. On the last and greatest
day of the Feast of Tabernacles, Jesus stood up and shouted his
identity. Finally some of the people began to get it and said,
"'Surely this man is the Prophet.' Others said, 'He is the Christ.'
Still others asked, 'How can the Christ come from Galilee?'"
(John 7:40–41).

Galilee, to the undiscerning, was not the place God would call
"home." The Jewish leaders were sure of this. When Nicodemus—
yes, *that* Nicodemus—asked his fellow Pharisees to at least listen
to what Jesus had to say, he was met with a challenge, "Are you
from Galilee, too? Look into it, and you will find that a prophet
does not come out of Galilee" (John 7:52).

The Jews were in the right place at the right time, but they
were so undiscerning that they were sure that it was really the
wrong place and the wrong time.

Jesus said it was the right place: The kingdom. But the people were convinced that Galilee couldn't be the right place. Jesus said it was the right time: Now. But the people were convinced that the Messiah couldn't have come because he was to come later.

Discernment is essential if we want to be impacted by God. Jesus came to change these people's lives, but because they weren't discerning correctly, they missed an opportunity to be changed by God.

How discerning are you? How often are you at the right place at the right time? Do you recognize when you are? Life can fly by at light-speed, or I should say *we* fly by life at light-speed. We race past right places and right times like mile markers on the highway. Those key opportunities where we could have been impacted by God or could have made an impact for God are lost in the blur.

It seems as if it were just yesterday that I was racing my Big Wheel up and down the driveway trying to beat Frank's Green Machine. Now I own a driveway.

It seems as if it were just yesterday I was playing basketball with my dad, amazed at his strength and skill. Now I'm playing basketball with my children.

It seems as if it were just yesterday that I was standing with a red-headed, Tennessee beauty dressed in white and was promising to love her until our bodies gave up this life. Now we're in our second decade of marriage.

 ## REFUEL!

1. Go to a local office supply store and purchase a wall calendar. Place a picture of your loved ones on the front of it. Put it in a place where you can see the picture each time you view the calendar.

2. Get together with your spouse and list the important events in the next year of your life. Make sure to list every special family activity, every birthday, every anniversary, and every occasion you can think of that would be tragic to miss.

3. Now, as a family, schedule regular family time at least once a month—in permanent black ink. Make this a priority and fight to protect this time.

4. Place a piece of paper on the refrigerator—for the family to see—and write in large letters the phrase, Be where the bein' is.

It seems as if it were just yesterday that my daughter was a newborn lying on my chest, sleeping peacefully while James Taylor serenaded us from the CD player in the corner of the hospital room as I smiled uncontrollably. Now she's two digits old!

The thing that is most disturbing to me about the *U.S. News and World Report* study I mentioned earlier in this chapter is that we will spend about five years of our lives waiting in line. I hate lines! When I think about most of the lines I find myself in, I realize that most of them lead nowhere. Or, rather, that they lead somewhere, but that somewhere is really nowhere significant.

I live in Orlando, the world of lines—Walt Disney World, Sea World, Hub Cap World. While you wait in line for popular rides at Disney World like Space Mountain, you'll find encouraging signs informing you how many minutes you have left to wait: *45-minute wait from this point.* For example, at Walt Disney's Magic Kingdom you'll typically wait ninety minutes for a ninety-second ride on Dumbo. Who's the real Dumbo?

Recently, my family and I went to Sea World. My wife had a great idea: we would just relax and enjoy each other. We decided not to ride any rides or wait in any lines, but to just hang out together in the playground and walk slowly through the park. What a great day! We weren't wasting time. We were bein' where the bein' is. We got out of line and discovered ourselves in the right place at the right time.

Do you need to get out of line? Look ahead and see if it's really worth the wait. If not, get out of line. Lines are deceptive. They seem to lead where the bein' is, but that rarely is true. If the line you're in is not leading to where the bein' is then get out of line.

Are you in line to work more?

Are you in line to earn more?

Are you in line to spend more?

Are you in line to travel more?

Are you in line to "be" more?

You're trapped when you're in line. Get out and you'll lose your position and have to go to the end of the line—if you choose to get back in line at all. But while in line, you can't be anywhere else, and often anywhere else is exactly where you need to be.

One father decided he needed to get out of his line in order to get his son in line.

It seems that in his early years of high school, James had something of a rebellious streak. He started getting into trouble at school. It was nothing overly serious, but enough to concern his parents. At the time, his father was a traveling evangelist. He was popular and well-respected among his particular denominational group. In fact, he was so popular that he was booked for revivals at least four years in advance. But when James started having problems, his father decided he needed to be more actively involved in parenting. He immediately cancelled all of his revivals and took a local pastorate. In the coming years, he spent much more time with James. A lot of that time was spent hunting and fishing. And today, if you have ever listened to James Dobson speak or have read any of his books, you know how big an influence his father had on his life. I can't prove it, but I'm personally convinced that all of the positive good that James Dobson and Focus on the Family has done for the families of our nation can be traced back to a father who experienced a conflict of priorities and made a hard decision. He decided to get out of line, and he obviously made the right decision.[2]

Discernment is essential if we want to be impactful for God. We all need to ask ourselves regularly, "Where's the bein'?"

At the dinner table tonight?

At your daughter's piano recital next week?

At your son's ballgame?

With your mother at the nursing home?

On the floor wrestling with the kids?

Helping a friend through a messy divorce?

Playing catch with the sons of a single mother?

On the couch next to your spouse—with the TV off?

Please get out of line and find the joy of bein' where the bein' is.

HOPE

At this, those who heard began to go away one at a time, the older ones first, until only Jesus was left, with the woman still standing there.

—John 8:9

I'm a skinny man who was always a skinny kid. I think I weighed about fifteen pounds in kindergarten. Bullies loved me.

One day while walking home from school carrying my books and wearing my hooded corduroy jacket, my world began to spin. Several fourth-grade boys had decided that day was the day I would die. One of the boys had me by the hood of my jacket and was spinning me around—and around. I saw my short, skinny life pass before my eyes. I began to feel hopeless when—all of a sudden—I heard her, and I knew that justice was on the way.

My sister Leigh-Angela was a sixth grader and a giant compared to me and my fourth-grade tormentors. She always looked out for me.

As the bullies were about to finish me off, my sister suddenly and powerfully appeared out of the bushes to save my life. These boys never knew what hit them.

Girls fight a little differently than boys. Boys typically use their hands and feet in a fight. My sister was a little more creative.

This was the early 70s, so she was wearing platform shoes that must have weighed about fifty pounds each. These shoes didn't just make a fashion statement; they were also a small part of the arsenal of weapons my sister used to save my life. I witnessed those shoes and every single part of my sister's body transform into lethal weapons. It was awesome!

You don't really want to mess with my sister.

In a victorious flurry my sister used her body to save my life and restore hope. Those bullies ran away and never picked on me again. The danger was gone, my hero was near, and fear had been replaced by hope.

Have you ever felt hopeless—like the bullies are winning and your hero is preoccupied somewhere else? The adulteress did … but she was about to see her hero drive her bullies away with one finger.

She had been caught in a bad situation. Can you see her? Hair disheveled. Eyes downcast. Cheeks moist and red from tears. Feet bare. Robe wrinkled and falling off of one shoulder. Humiliated. Ashamed. Judged. Guilty. Hopeless.

She had been caught in the very act of adultery and she was in trouble. The bullies were determined to hurt her. Her world was spinning and she could see the stones. The Bullisees (Bully + Pharisee = Bullisee) and teachers of the Law didn't care about her; she was irrelevant. She was only bait in a trap set for Jesus.

These Jewish leaders didn't fight fair. They had twisted God's Law into a hideous weapon that they often used to destroy the weak, the hurting, and the helpless. These thugs had been bullying people for a long time and very few people would stand up to them. It seemed that this woman was in big trouble.

The Pharisees and teachers of the Law knew that the Law of Moses was very explicit when it came to adultery: both the adulterer and the adulteress must be put to death (see Lev. 20:10). Yet they did not bring the guilty man because he was irrelevant, too. Their purpose wasn't to obey the Law. The only reason this woman was brought to Jesus was to trap him in front of a large crowd of people. If Jesus didn't recommend that she be stoned to death according to the Law, then the Pharisees would accuse him of being a traitor to the Old Testament. If Jesus sentenced her to death, then they would kill her and report him to the Roman authorities. The Romans had forbidden anyone but Rome from carrying out the death penalty. The Jewish leaders thought that Jesus was in an inescapable trap.

They were wrong.

These hypocrites asked the author of the Law, "Teacher, this woman was caught in the act of adultery. In the Law Moses commanded us to stone such women. Now what do you say?" (John 8:4–5).

These Bullisees and teachers of the law didn't care about the answer to this question. They knew the answer, and they knew that Jesus knew the answer, too.

Remember this: the problem with legalists is not that they love the Law too much, but that they love people too little. Jesus loves people more than he loves anything else. Jesus loved this woman so much that he replaced the fear in her heart with hope. These Jewish leaders saw a broken Law; Jesus saw a broken person who needed to be restored.

In answer to the question, Jesus bent down and began to write in the ground with his finger, seemingly ignoring the bullies. They wouldn't quit. They kept swinging her around by her hood. So he stood up for her.

Do you know that Jesus will always stand up for you? When the bullies have you surrounded, he will stand up for you. When your enemies stand with anger in their hearts and stones in their hands, he will stand up for you. When you feel like you're standing alone in your fear, he will stand up for you. He loves you.

He loved her, too, so he spoke up for her as well. Jesus said, "If any one of you is without sin, let him be the first to throw a stone at her" (John 8:7), and then he stooped down and wrote in the ground again.

What in the world did the Word write? This is the only time in the Bible that we read of Jesus writing, so you'd think we'd be told what he wrote. We're not … so we speculate. But maybe we aren't told what he wrote because we know what it read: "Hope."

With one finger and a few words, Jesus drove the bullies away. They dropped their stones and left her alone. Jesus then stood up for her again and asked her, "'Woman, where are they? Has no one condemned you?' 'No one, sir,' she said. 'Then neither do I condemn you,' Jesus declared. 'Go now and leave your life of sin'" (John 8:10–11). I bet she skipped away.

I love a happy ending. With one finger and some dirt, the damsel in distress has been saved and hope has been reborn in her soul. Cue the music and roll the credits.

But before we leave this event, let me make sure you saw what happened. In this one encounter Jesus actually saved her twice: once from stones and once from sin. Jesus wanted her to know true hope, and true hope isn't just physical, it's spiritual as well.

Do you have true hope?

True hope has nothing to do with how much money you have in the bank.

True hope has nothing to do with a big office, a nice house, or a car that doesn't break down.

True hope is not found in a health club, a night club, or a social club.

True hope is not found in a great insurance or pension plan.

True hope has nothing to do with your physical health or life circumstances.

In fact, you can be seriously ill and still have hope.

You can be surrounded by poverty and still have hope.

You can be surrounded by abuse and still have hope.

You can be surrounded by heartache and still have hope.

You can even be surrounded by certain death and still have hope.

All this is true if you remember that Jesus loves you, died for you, and rose for you, so that he could ultimately rescue you for eternity.

He's not just doodling in the sand while the bullies surround you, threaten you, and swing you around by your hood … he's writing a message to you and a warning to the bullies … and it reads, *Hope.*

◪ REFUEL!

1. List the five biggest problems that you feel surrounded by right now:

a) _____

b) _____

c) _____

d) _____

e) _____

2. Take this list outside and find a place with some exposed dirt.

3. Sit down, read John 8, and reflect on the hope that you have in Christ as you face these "bullies."

4. Now, with your finger, write the word hope *in the dirt.*

5. Recite this simple prayer:

> Lord, you know the problems that bully me each day (state each of the five biggest problems you listed above). Sometimes these problems are so oppressive. Sometimes I feel like they are spinning me around and are going to defeat me, but they are not going to win. Lord, I trust you and I know that you will not allow me to be defeated. Lord, help me to be strong; help me to be brave.

They are not going to win. Lord, I trust you and I know that you will not allow me to be defeated. Lord, help me to be strong, help me to be brave, and Lord, please help me to place my hope—not in the things of this world, but in you. Amen.

6. Repeat as necessary.

VISION

One thing I do know. I was blind but now I see!

—*John 9:25*

My son Levi was only sixteen months old, but he was already using his imagination. One day he started pretending he was blind. He would walk around the room with his eyes closed, waving his hands in the air, but with a big smile on his face. It was really cute. But blindness in real life isn't cute—it's tragic. Imagine the challenges of living in a personal world of darkness.

Jesus understood those challenges, so physical blindness was something that he healed while here on earth. He also healed spiritual blindness during his ministry. On at least one occasion, he healed both at once.

In the ninth chapter of John, we find that Jesus was surrounded by a bunch of blind people: one physically blind man, twelve blind disciples, and a bunch of blind Pharisees.

As Jesus walked along, he saw a man who was blind from birth. His disciples asked, "Who sinned and caused this man to be born blind?" They were blind to this man's physical need because all they could see was an opportunity to learn a little more theology. It's as if the disciples were saying, "Lord, we think we've got it figured out. Let us impress you by asking a really impressive theological question that shows you we are smart." Jesus was not impressed or deterred by this self-serving attempt to impress him with a deep theological-type question that was only to make them look like they were desiring to learn about the things of God.

Are we guilty of this? Are we blind to the hurting people we pass on our way to church? Are we blind to the hurting people who live next door to the home where we have our small group? Are we blind to the depressed coworker we rush past so we can make it to mid-week Bible study on time?

We must not let our love for learning more about the Creator keep us from loving the people he created. We also must not mistake a love of knowledge about God with love for God. Knowing about God is not the same as knowing God. One who knows about God can recite a dozen Scriptures about helping hurting people. One who knows God helps dozens of hurting people.

Jesus doesn't take this opportunity to criticize his blind buddies for their momentary lapse of vision but instead carefully answers their question. His answer was that this man's blindness was not a penalty for sin, but an opportunity for power.

Jesus had a plan, and it involved using spit, mud, and a pool. (Author's note: You're about to encounter one of the coolest healings in the Bible. Being a guy, I am drawn by forces within me that I can't really explain to any Bible story that condones spitting on any level.) Jesus spat on the ground and made some mud balls. He put these mud balls on the blind man's eyes and told him to wash in the Pool of Siloam. I'm sure the man couldn't understand how this would work, but he obeyed, washed, and "came home seeing" (John 9:7).

One blind man down, many more to go.

His friends and neighbors couldn't believe what they were witnessing. Some recognized him and others didn't, which left the now-seeing man (formerly known to them only as "a man blind from birth") to insist, "I am the man" (John 9:9). He's really

saying, "Look at me! Can't you see me? I am that man you felt
sorry for. I'm the one you stepped over and around. You haven't
seen me in years, but you must look at me now!"

To which his friends and neighbors replied, "How did this
happen? And who did this to you?" No one said,
"Congratulations!" No one said, "That's great news." No one
asked, "Do you like what clouds look like?" No one asked,
"Aren't camels funny looking?" No one exclaimed, "I've got to
show you something!" Instead, they were more concerned with
bringing to justice the man who had broken the Law by healing
on the Sabbath, so they took the seeing man to the local school of
the spiritually blind: the synagogue.

When Jesus healed this blind man, he spat in the eyes of the
legalistic Pharisees who were so blinded by their power that they
could no longer see the powerless around them. That power
came from the Law, so they fought desperately and often irra-
tionally to protect every letter of the Law. Jesus had healed this
blind man on the Sabbath. The Pharisees considered any act,
even restoring sight to blind eyes, to be work, and working on
the Sabbath was a violation of the Law.

So the newly seeing man, who should have been joyfully wan-
dering around looking at stuff, found himself under attack by those
who could not see. After a second interrogation, the seeing man
testified once and for all, "Whether he is a sinner or not, I don't
know. One thing I do know. I was blind but now I see!" (John 9:25).

The Pharisees didn't get it and wouldn't get it. Their blindness was spiritual, not physical, and that's much harder to heal.
It was going to take a lot more than dirt and spit to restore their
vision. Their spiritual blindness was so severe and had so cor-
rupted them that they were attacking an innocent man. They
challenged him, insulted him, labeled him a sinner, and then
threw him out of the synagogue (see John 9:34).

Why were the Pharisees so angry with this innocent man?
They were afraid. They felt threatened by Jesus and by what he

had done for the formerly blind man. They saw what was happening and knew that it must be stopped. If Jesus were free to minister unhindered, then his physical healings combined with his "radical" words would liberate untold multitudes of people from spiritual blindness. The spiritually blind are threatened by those with vision. Those with vision go places that the blind will never go. Those with vision see things that the blind will never see. Those with vision dream dreams that the blind won't ever understand. The only thing the spiritually blind know to do when confronted with a visionary is to challenge him, insult him, and—if nothing else works—throw him out of the church.

Are you blind? Can you see?

Jesus wants you to have vision and he wants you to see. He wants you to open spiritual eyes and glimpse the glorious future he has designed just for you. Vision is one of the elements of an abundant life, and it is essential.

The blind man's healing shows us three things that can cause us to go spiritually blind:

DARKNESS

> "As long as it is day, we must do the work of him who sent me. Night is coming, when no one can work." (John 9:4)

Close your eyes. What do you see? The world of the blind man was full of darkness. His world was dark physically; it was also spiritually dark. He was surrounded by heartless hypocrites who couldn't and wouldn't see him as he sat begging for some of their monetary attention. This depth of darkness can blind. Creatures that dwell in darkness too long eventually lose their vision. The darkest parts of a cave and deepest parts of the ocean are home to creatures that no longer can see.

Jesus said that "night is coming, when no one can work." In the ancient world, work typically ended with the setting sun. No light, no work. Darkness blinds and makes work impossible. We must make it a point to avoid spiritual darkness because God has a vision for our lives and work for us to do.

In *God Came Near*, Max Lucado tells the story of a man's escape from darkness. For fifty-one years, Bob Edens was blind. He couldn't see a thing. His world was a black hall of sounds and smells. He felt his way through five decades of darkness. And then, he could see. A skilled surgeon performed a complicated operation and, for the first time, Bob Edens had sight. He found it overwhelming. "I never would have dreamed that yellow is so ... yellow," he exclaimed. "I don't have the words. I am amazed by yellow. But red is my favorite color. I just can't believe red. I can see the shape of the moon—and I like nothing better than seeing a jet plane flying across the sky leaving a vapor trail. And of course, sunrises and sunsets. And at night I look at the stars in the sky and the flashing light. You could never know how wonderful everything is."[1] Vision is a wonderful thing.

DIRT

> "The man they call Jesus made some mud and put it on my eyes. He told me to go to Siloam and wash. So I went and washed, and then I could see." (John 9:11)

Dirt can blind. On November 30, 1991, fierce winds from a freakish dust storm triggered a massive auto pileup along Interstate 5 near Coalinga, California. At least fourteen people died and dozens more were injured as topsoil whipped by fifty-mile-per-hour winds reduced visibility to zero. That afternoon's holocaust left a three-mile trail of twisted and burning vehicles, some stacked on top of one another hundred yards from the freeway. Unable to see their way, dozens of motorists blindly drove ahead into disaster.

The dirt in this event was physical dirt, but we can be blinded just as easily by spiritual dirt. What happens to us before we go to sleep? We shower. We brush our teeth. We put on clean pajamas and crawl into fresh-smelling, cool, crisp, white, cotton sheets. But when we wake up in the morning, it's like we've been up all night mud wrestling. We have bad breath, body odor, and globs of gunk in the corners of our eyes. To see clearly throughout the day, this gunk must be cleaned out.

Clear vision is so important that God designed tears to keep our eyes clean from the dust, pollen, dirt, and debris floating around us that constantly contaminates us. In his Sermon on the Mount, Christ taught us not only the importance of keeping our spiritual eyes clean but also the impact dirty spiritual eyes can have on the rest of our body:

> "If your right eye causes you to sin, gouge it out and throw it away." (Matt. 5:29)

> "The eye is the lamp of the body. If your eyes are good, your whole body will be full of light. But if your eyes are bad, your whole body will be full of darkness." (Matt. 6:22–23)

DEGENERATION

> Some Pharisees who were with him heard him say this and asked, "What? Are we blind too?" (John 9:40)

Physical degeneration can lead to blindness. According to the organization Prevent Blindness America, Glaucoma and macular degeneration, two leading causes of physical blindness, "will double their impact in the coming years as the nation's seventy-six million baby boomers reach older adulthood. This dramatic increase in age-related eye disease threatens to overwhelm the nation's health care resources and diminish the quality of life for millions. In fact, by the year 2030 there will be twice as many blind people as today. Macular degeneration will continue to be the leading cause of blindness. And there will be a near doubling of the total cases of glaucoma."[2]

Spiritual degeneration can lead to spiritual blindness. Degeneration means, "To decline in quality." The Pharisees had declined in quality as religious leaders. The Pharisees were a prominent religious party in Judaism from about 100 BC to AD 70. Our word for *pharisee* is a transliteration of their name in Greek (*pharisaioi*), which means "separated ones." They were supposed to be separated from the governments of this world and from worldly sins. Pharisees were a Jewish party who voluntarily undertook a strict regimen of purity laws, observance of the Sabbath, prayer, and tithing. A Pharisee was usually a layman without scribal education. The Pharisees observed and perpetuated an oral tradition of the Law, handed down from the former teachers and wise men of Israel. This oral Law—called Halakah—was a strict list of rules governing purity, fasting, tithing, prayer, and worship. The Pharisees were the most prominent of the three Jewish societies, which included the Sadducees and the Essenes. Pharisees were found everywhere in Palestine. At their highest point, there were about 6,000 Pharisees there. Pharisees were committed to both religious and social purity. They strongly opposed the influence of Greek paganism in their world and felt superior to other nations. But the Pharisees missed the point of righteousness.

In the New Testament, the word *Pharisee* is used almost synonymously with *hypocrite*. These men were concerned about minor details of the Law, yet apathetic toward the needs of people. They were so focused on protecting the Law that they had forgotten the importance of living the life they promoted.

Through the blind man's healing, we see how much the Pharisees had degenerated. They cared more about holy days than hurting people. The Sabbath was worth fighting for; the blind were not. They cared more about punishing Christ than helping people. They had become spiritually blind and lost sight of the vision that God had for them. We must not let that happen to us.

My dad was an amazing man. I don't remember ever seeing him cry, but I know he did. In 1988, he found out that something

◪ REFUEL!

1. *Watch the movie* Patch Adams *featuring Robin Williams.*

2. *As you watch this film, reflect on how Patch becomes a hero to his patients. How is this similar to Christ?*

3. *In one scene of the movie, Patch visits his mentor in his office. Patch's medical school teacher asks Patch to hold up his hand. He then asks Patch, "How many fingers do you see?" Patch answers, "Four?" What is significant about what happens next?*

4. *Reflect on this question: In general, as you live this life, how many fingers do you see?*

was destroying his eyes. He was a teacher, a preacher, a writer, and a reader, and the doctors predicted that he would go blind. He put an eye chart on the mirror in his bathroom and did all he could do to save his eyesight. My mom later told me that he was really scared to go blind and spent time praying and crying before the Lord. On August 8, 1988, my dad died of a heart attack while taking a nap. The time of death was about 1:44 p.m. At 1:45 p.m., he wasn't going blind anymore. At that very moment, he saw the Lord. I wonder what my dad's first conversation with Christ was like. They loved each other so much. I may be wrong, but I think it went something like this: "Roger, it's so good to see you!" To which Dad replied, "Jesus, it's good to SEE you too."

He didn't let the *darkness* of this world blind him.

He didn't let the *dirt* in this world blind him.

He didn't let the *degeneration* of this world blind him.

What about you? Are you blind? God wants to restore your vision.

SUBMISSION

I am the good shepherd; I know my sheep and my sheep know me ...
and I lay down my life for the sheep.

—*John 10:14–15*

Tundra liked to run away. She was a beautiful dog who joined our family as a puppy. We loved her, but I was never quite sure the feeling was mutual. I didn't understand it. She had a great yard, good food, and fresh water, yet if she found a hole in the fence or an open gate, she was gone. As a Siberian Husky, Tundra was designed to run, so whenever she broke free we knew it was going to be for a while. As a result, I spent too much time chasing her when I would have rather been loving her.

I don't know why she would run. In her yard she was safe and secure, but out in the world she faced many dangers. My goal was to keep her safe; her goal seemed to be to run away from that safety.

So why did she run? Simply because I had not trained her to submit. So when she would get out, I would do what I was supposed to do—shout, "Stop! Sit! Heel! Please, in the name of all that's holy, would you at least slow down!"—but she wouldn't cooperate. As she disappeared into the horizon, I could almost hear her yelping, *"You're not the boss of me!"*

Sound familiar? Submission problems are not limited to animals. Four-year-old children can have submission problems. Even fifty-four-year-old adults can have submission problems. So I wasn't surprised to hear my daughter proclaim to her friend, "You're not the boss of me!" I've said it, and I'm sure you've said it, too. It's a classic line born out of the fall of man.

It's a cry for power, control, and liberation. "Who are you to tell me what to do?" We don't like to be told what to do, and we don't like to submit our will to the will of another.

Do you ever find yourself thinking or saying, "You're not the boss of me!"? Does it flow through your heart when your boss confronts you about a problem in your department? Does it move to the tip of your tongue when your mother-in-law offers you her "opinion" about how to keep your child from throwing a tantrum? Do you sometimes feel like whispering it loudly to your spouse when you're navigating through busy traffic? Does it ever well up in your heart in the midst of a sermon at church?

Submission has become a dirty word in our do-whatever-I-want-whenever-I-want-and-no-one-can-tell-me-it's-wrong society. But submission is a fundamental word in the lexicon of Christianity. Since that first day in the first garden, God has expected us to submit to his will. And since that first bite of forbidden fruit, we've stood up to God or yelled over our shoulders as we ran in the opposite direction or proclaimed through our choices, "You're not the boss of me!"

Nevertheless, submission is an element of abundant life

 ## REFUEL!

1. List the top five things you've done in your life that failed. Then list one thing that God has done that has failed.

2. Based on this information, who is best qualified to be in charge of your life?

because submission to God is a key to our survival. He is bigger, stronger, better, and wiser than we. He stands guard over us, protects us, and provides for us. He is like a shepherd, and we are like sheep.

The events of John 10 occurred just before the Feast of Dedication, which was in the winter. Christ would be on the cross by the spring. Jesus knew that his friends—his disciples—were going to see him die soon, so he prepared them for the difficult task of independent obedience. In order to do what Christ needed them to do after his ascension into heaven, his disciples would have to be able to follow an unseen leader. This would require submission of the will—submission to the Good Shepherd.

Good shepherds are essential for a flock's survival because by nature sheep are defenseless, weak, and—from what I've been told—stupid. My dad worked shearing sheep when he was a teen. He told me that it was not uncommon to catch sheep doing stupid things. One day he saw a line of sheep approach a shrub. The first sheep jumped the shrub. The next sheep also jumped, but was not quite next to the shrub, so the jump wasn't really needed. This routine continued down the line as each sheep jumped, even though the line continually moved farther away from the shrub.

Sheep have a much better chance of surviving in this world if they have a shepherd, especially a good shepherd. A good shepherd leads his sheep to green pastures so they can eat and rest. A good shepherd stands between his sheep and danger. A good shepherd watches over the sheep as they sleep. A good shepherd enhances the life of submissive sheep.

Jesus gave two reasons why we sheep should submit to our Good Shepherd. First, he knows us. John wrote, "The watchman opens the gate for him, and the sheep listen to his voice. He calls his own sheep by name and leads them out" (10:3). How do you feel when someone you've only recently met calls you by name? Don't you feel special when you realize in amazement, *He remembered me* or *She knows who I am?* It feels good to be known. The Creator of all things knows us by name. That's cool. It's good to hear someone speak your name—especially when you know he or she cares about you. God loves you and shouts your name across a crowded world hoping you'll hear. Look his way and follow him. Jesus reminded us that "strangers" will try to lure us away, with a voice we won't recognize, so we have to be careful. This leads to the second reason we should submit to our Good Shepherd: he loves us.

In second grade, my daughter Ashton came home from school with news that was exciting to her, but disturbing to me. Her campus had to be locked down when a "Danger Stranger," or someone who could be a threat to the kids, was noticed close to the campus. The gates were closed, the doors were locked, the playground was emptied, and the hearts of the students were filled with fear by the thought that a bad person was close by. We've trained our kids to be aware that not all people are good and that some bad people will try to lure good children to a bad place with deceitful questions or promises. Jesus warned his disciples that whether or not they knew it, many thieves and robbers had been after them for some time, so they must be on their guard. He then warned that the ultimate "Danger Stranger" was lurking close by and wanted to "steal, kill, and destroy" them (John 10:10).

"Danger Strangers" are a hazard because their intentions are unclear. God's intentions are clear: he wants to lead us to a safe place where we will experience "life, and have it to the full" (John 10:10). So we would be wise to listen for his voice and submit to what he's telling us to do.

Wise sheep don't have submission problems. Well-fed sheep don't have submission problems. Protected sheep—who won't be eaten by wolves—don't have submission problems.

Despite what we may think, feel, or do, we must never forget how blessed we are to have Jesus as the boss of us.

TRANSFORMATION

Lazarus, come out!
—*John 11:43*

Makeovers make for good TV. Originally, TV makeovers involved people getting new clothes, an updated haircut, and some professional makeup. Somewhere along the line, personal makeovers got more involved and expensive. On TV shows like "Extreme Makeover," we now see personal makeovers in which the people get new faces, new teeth, and new bodies through plastic surgery.

Personal makeovers are so popular that they are no longer limited to people. If we want to watch room makeovers, we can watch the Learning Channel's show *Trading Spaces*. If we want to see makeovers involving entire homes, we can watch *Extreme Makeover: Home Edition*. It seems that there are makeover shows for everyone and everything.

 ## REFUEL!

1. Stop and—before reading any further—watch a makeover show.
2. Which show did you watch?

> *3. In your opinion was the makeover successful? Why, or why not?*
>
> *4. How many makeover shows can you list?*
>
> *5. If you were to start a makeover show what would it be called? Why?*

Why are we so fascinated with makeovers? We love to see the joy that people receive from positive transformation. We love to see a sad woman in tattered jeans transformed into a beaming princess in a shimmering gown. We love to see the look on her husband's face and the gleam in his eye when he sees her new look for the first time. It makes us feel good to see changes that make people happy.

God loves makeovers, too. He loves to help us make healthy change in our lives, and he loves to see the joy that we receive from our positive transformation. He loves to see the look on our faces the first time we understand forgiveness, and he loves to see the look on the faces of our family and friends when they first see the change he has made in our lives. He loves to see broken hearts repaired, shattered dreams restored, divided families reunited, lost people saved, and dead people resurrected.

Let me tell you the story of Lazarus.

Lazarus was dead. Experts had said so. He had been wrapped up never to be unwrapped again ... but then he moved. Lazarus was a young beagle who lived in Duluth, Georgia. He was hit by a car in January 2004 and picked up as roadkill by the sanitation department. He was wrapped in a bag and sent to the local humane department to be incinerated. Just before his cremation, the shelter director checked to see if Lazarus matched the description of any missing pets. As she began to check him, he moved. He had suffered a brain injury, but after three days, he was on his feet and could walk, although only in circles to the right with his tongue hanging out and a dazed look in his eyes. In the online article, the director said that it was the first time in fourteen years of handling dead animals that she'd ever seen this happen.[1]

Let me tell you the story of another Lazarus who had also been wrapped up to be unwrapped no more.

Like you, Christ had close personal friends whom he deeply loved. One such friend was Lazarus. One day Mary and Martha, Lazarus's sisters, sent word to Jesus that "the one you love is sick" (John 11:3). They were certain that Jesus would immediately rush to Bethany and heal their brother, his friend. But he didn't. He waited two days and then went to Bethany, arriving after Lazarus had been dead and in the tomb for four days.

Why did Jesus wait in Peraea[2] when his friend was dying a few miles away in Judea? The answer is found in the first words out of his mouth after he heard that his best friend was sick: "This sickness will not end in death. No, it is for God's glory so that God's Son may be glorified through it" (John 11:4). And the answer is also found in what Jesus told his disciples after trying to explain Lazarus's death in terms of sleep: "Lazarus is dead, and for your sake I am glad I was not there, so that you may believe" (John 11:14–15). Jesus waited to go back because he knew that in raising Lazarus from the dead, he would also be raising Mary and Martha, his disciples, and us from the dead. He wasn't just interested in transforming Lazarus's life; he wanted to transform our lives as well.

Jesus waited because he didn't just want to do a makeover to impress us; he wanted to do an "extreme makeover" to transform us.

When Jesus arrived in Bethany, Martha ran out to meet him. She respectfully acknowledged that if he had come when they asked for him, then Lazarus would not have died.

Confidently, Jesus promised that her brother would be transformed: "Your brother will rise again" (John 11:23). Just as confidently Martha responded, "I know he will rise again in the resurrection at the last day" (John 11:24). But Jesus wasn't talking about the last day; he was talking about that very day. Jesus responded, "I am the resurrection and the life. He who believes in me will live, even though he dies; and whoever lives and believes in me will never die. Do you believe this?" (John 11:25–26).

Do you believe this? Do you believe that Jesus has the power to transform your life and death this way?

Jesus does have the power to transform your life ... today! Today, through belief in Christ, you can be transformed from a person sentenced to death into a person destined for eternal life.

Okay, I can hear what you're thinking: *I've messed up my life too much. There's no way anyone could forgive me for what I've done. I don't think there's any way out of the mess I'm in. My life is too messed up to be fixed any day ... especially today.*

We must remember that with Jesus there is always hope of transformation. Don't believe me? Just ask Lazarus. He'd probably tell you that four days in a tomb can really mess you up.

Bear with me while I try to help you to understand why Lazarus's makeover was truly an "extreme" makeover. (If you're hungry, you might want to go ahead and eat before you read this. If you've already eaten, you may want to wait at least a half an hour before you swim through this section. If you're reading this on a full stomach and you just don't care, remember that I warned you.)

Lazarus was Jewish. The Jewish custom during the time of Christ was to bury the person within twenty-four hours. Lazarus's body would not have been embalmed, but would have been washed, wrapped in linen, and possibly covered with spices before being buried in the tomb.

Without embalming, decay begins immediately upon

death. Each of us has bacteria that are constantly feeding on the contents of our intestines and are controlled as long as our bodies are alive. Immediately upon Lazarus's death these intestinal bacteria in his body—no longer under control—began to feed on his intestines. These bacteria then proceeded on to the rest of his major organs. Once the digestive fluids were released from these organs into the rest of his body, the decaying process became more rapid. By the fourth day after his death, the decaying organs would have been releasing a variety of gases that would cause his body to begin putrefaction. The smell of his body would have been considered foul by all except the insects that would have already taken up refuge in and begun feeding on his body.

Get the picture? (I warned you.)

So you see, Martha displayed wisdom and a great deal of common sense when she tried to deter Jesus from removing the stone that covered Lazarus's tomb by stating, "by this time there is a bad odor, for he has been there four days" (John 11:39).

Undeterred, Jesus offered a prayer and then issued a challenge to his dead, decaying, and probably very smelly friend— "Lazarus, come out!" (John 11:43). And he did.

Jesus called. Lazarus obeyed and was immediately transformed from one who was dead to one who was alive again.

What were you saying about being a lost cause beyond the hope of transformation? If Jesus can transform a four-days-dead-and-decaying man into a walking, talking, eating, and potentially skipping healthy man, then he can certainly transform your life as well.

Today, Jesus is calling you to positive transformation, too. He's calling you to come out of your tomb of fear. He's calling you to come out of your tomb of addiction. He's calling you to come out of your tomb of sin. He's calling you to come out of your tomb of selfishness. He's calling you to come out of your tomb of death and be resurrected for all eternity. As long as you are still breathing it's not too late to come out of your tomb and be transformed.

Recently, I read about a thirty-nine-year-old Ashland, Massachusetts woman who was wrongly pronounced dead and zipped into a body bag—only to awaken later in a funeral parlor. Police officers had been called to her house to investigate a blaring radio. When they entered the apartment, they found the woman lying in a partially filled bathtub. She did not appear to be breathing and had no discernible pulse. They found a bottle of pills and a suicide note nearby. She showed no signs of life, so the woman—who was not dead, but suffering from a drug overdose and hypothermia—ended up in a body bag instead of in an ambulance. She received emergency medical treatment only after the frightened funeral home director heard breathing coming from inside the body bag. The woman recovered, but Massachusetts Department of Public Health officials launched an inquiry into whether the EMTs on the scene provided the woman with proper care.

There was one quote from a doctor that should give all of us hope. Dr. Murray Hamlet, a hypothermia resuscitation expert in Natick, Massachusetts, said, "The fact that they didn't take her to the hospital, just assumed she was dead, is the big mistake. People have to understand that cold, stiff, blue people can be resuscitated."[3]

Did you catch that last line? That's exactly what Jesus wanted us to learn from Lazarus because it's not just true physically—it's true spiritually as well. When you feel like road kill, remember with Jesus there's always hope. Jesus is standing and calling for you to "Come Out!" Will you? It's not too late. Even one who is spiritually cold, stiff, and blue can be transformed.

◩ REFUEL!

1. I want you to pray the following prayer at least one time a day for the next thirty days.

Lord, transform me. Amen.

2. How did God transform your life in the last thirty days? Be specific.

3. I know that after thirty days you have only just begun to change, but it's a start!

PASSION

Why wasn't this perfume sold and the money given to the poor?

—John 12:5

One of my first encounters with passion was in fourth grade. Her name was Sheila, and she looked like a goddess. When she walked into the classroom, I could hear the angels singing and see light radiating from around her. She was what the poets would call, "Hot."

PASSION IS AN INTENSE EMOTION THAT COMPELS ACTION.

Valentine's Day was a big day in elementary school. We would hang envelopes on the corners of our desks and then get in line and file by our classmates' desks, willingly and lovingly placing valentines into each envelope. I remember the Valentine's Day that changed my life—February 14, 1979. Sheila floated by my desk, smiled, and dropped her valentine slowly into my carefully decorated manila envelope. As she passed, my heart stopped.

After school, I rushed home, threw open the door, ignored the candy, and searched for the ultimate prize: Sheila's valentine. When I read it, I knew that there was a God and that he loved me because she had signed it, *Love, Sheila*.

She loved me!

Passion!

Passion is powerful. Passion is also transformational. Passion can transform ordinary to extraordinary, good to great, and a life that's busy to a life that's abundant because passion does two things:

PASSION MAKES OUR LIVES IMPORTANT.

My passion for Sheila brought poetry out of my heart and onto the lined paper of my spiral notebook. My passion for Sheila inspired me to carry her books as we walked through the halls. My passion for Sheila even kept me from hitting her with the red ball during dodge ball, instead taking aim at my best friend, Frank. My passion for Sheila drove me to write her name on my desk ... fifty times.

Passion will drive grown men to yell at the TV, mature women to scream like schoolgirls, and sane adults to act like fools. Passion can drive us to do things that are not only irrational but are unimportant. We often exert our passion on things that don't matter: sports, entertainment, and pleasure. Wasted passion satisfies neither us, nor God.

Frank Stoeber of Cawker City, Kansas was a passionate man. He learned of the existence of the World's Largest Ball of Twine (twelve feet and 21,140 pounds) in Darwin, Minnesota, so he set out to beat it. Day after day, week after week, and year after year, he worked passionately to roll the new World's Largest Ball of Twine, but he died when his ball was still one foot too small. In his honor, the city officials of his hometown put Frank's passion on display as the "Second Largest Ball of Twine." What will be on display from your life after you are gone? Are you doing important things?

Our passion can also drive us to do things that are seemingly irrational but are actually very important.

Passion convicts us to stop putting off what we know needs to be done.

Passion gets us out of bed at 5:00 AM to run three miles.

Passion enrolls us in night school.

Passion sends us home from work early so we can go to a park and swing with the kids.

Passion drives us to the hospital in the middle of the night to pray with a sick friend.

Passion prompts calls to our spouses at work just to say, "I was thinking about you."

REFUEL!

1. Watch the movie The Rookie *featuring Dennis Quaid.*
2. What was Jim Morris passionate about? Reflect on the sacrifices he made to follow his passion. Would you have given up?
3. What are you passionate about? Is God passionate about what you're passionate about? If so, what would you be willing to sacrifice to follow that passion?

In the opening verses of John 12, we are told of a woman driven by passion. What she did was completely sane and insane all at the same time. During this time in history, it was completely sane and socially appropriate to give a dinner in honor of someone. It was also completely sane and socially appropriate to have your lowliest servant wash the feet of an honored guest in your home. Journeys were long, days were hot, roads were dusty, and Odor Eaters were still millennia away. But, it was completely insane to wash your guests' smelly feet with your life's savings! John tells us that this perfume was worth about a year's wages. Since the average American makes about $35,000 a year, by today's standards, Mary essentially anointed Jesus with a Lexus.

Mary poured this very expensive perfume on Christ's

calluses because of passion. She rubbed her clean hair on his dirty feet because of passion. She had passion to serve the man who called her brother out of the tomb. She had that passion because Jesus had changed her life. She had that passion because he had given her hope. She had passion for the man who was going to die. Mary's passion drove her to anoint Christ with perfume that was valued at a year's wages. This didn't make sense.

Was this wasted passion? Judas thought so. He objected and said, "Why wasn't this perfume sold and the money given to the poor?" (John 12:5).

Lazarus was there, but he didn't complain. It seemed appropriate to him.

Martha was there, but she didn't complain because she was too busy to notice.

Jesus was there—his feet covered with perfume—and he thought it was wonderful. He praised her for her passion and predicted that we would praise her (see Matt. 26:13). Mary's passion was not a waste because she had allowed it to motivate an act that seemed irrational but was actually very important.

What are you passionate about? Is what you're passionate about really important?

Once, Jesus was asked the important question. Not *an* important question, but *the* important question. An expert in the Law tested Jesus with a question, "Teacher, which command in God's Law is the most important?" Jesus said, "'Love the Lord your God with all your passion and prayer and intelligence.' This is the most important, the first on any list" (Matt. 22:34–38 MSG). God wants us to love him with every cell of our body. Passion for God is the most important answer to the most important question because if we get this right, then we'll get everything else right.

Passion is transforming because it makes our life important, but it's also transforming because …

PASSION MAKES OUR LIFE IMPACTFUL (YES, I MADE UP THIS WORD).

That's what we learn as we read Christ's answer to the big question the expert in the Law didn't ask but should have: what's really important to God? This is the question we all should ask. Jesus taught us that God wants us to be passionate for him so that we'll be passionate for people. Jesus continued, "But there is a second to set alongside it: 'Love others as well as you love yourself.' These two commands are pegs; everything in God's Law and the Prophets hangs from them" (Matt. 22:39–40 MSG).

If we are passionate for God, then we'll be passionate for what's really important: people. If we are passionate for God, then we will impact the lives of others by loving them.

Want to love your spouse more? Love God more.

Want to love your kids more? Love God more.

Want to love your parents more? Love God more.

Want to love your boss more? (Yes, you just read what you think you just read! Want to love your boss more?) Then love God more.

Passion for God will change your life and the lives of people around you.

John remembered this foot washing in such detail that we can almost see Mary's act of passion … and smell it! "Mary took about a pint of pure nard, an expensive perfume; she poured it on Jesus' feet and wiped his feet with her hair. *And the house was filled with the fragrance of the perfume*" (John 12:3).

This reminds me of coming home from elementary school. My struggles with adverbs, bullies, and a long walk home were always quickly forgotten when the smell of chocolate chip cookies greeted me as I walked in the door. I never doubted my mother's love for me, but on the days she made cookies, her love was so powerful I could smell it. Mom's passion for her family impacted my life.

Does your passion impact the lives of those around you?

Jesus could smell Mary's love. The disciples could smell Mary's love. I can almost smell her love today. Mary's act of passion was not just important, it was also impactful.

I once heard Calvin Miller tell the story of when he was a teenager working on his sister's farm in Pond Creek, Oklahoma, and the First Christian Church of Pond Creek caught fire. He said that the scene was surreal as people stumbled out of the darkness of their homes and into the light of the flickering flames. From behind doors, faces emerged that had not been seen in years. People presumed dead and gone were seen alive and well. Old Farmer Henderson and Old Farmer Johnson—who hadn't spoken to each other in years—now stood side-by-side in front of the fire chatting, in the way only farmers can chat:

"That's a big fire."

"Yup."

The flames of the church beckoned slumbering souls to wake up and lonesome souls to leave the solitude of their homes and "be where the bein' was." Everybody stood and watched that church burn to the ground because they knew the fire would change their lives.

It's a proven fact: when churches burn, they attract a crowd and impact the lives of all who gather to watch them burn. When we burn with passion, we will impact the lives of others, too. Calvin Miller closed his story with the words of John Wesley: "Catch on fire with enthusiasm and people will come from miles to watch you burn."

Don't be ordinary. Live an important life. Live an impactful life. Live a passion-filled life. It's not a waste.

I recently read an article that after Frank Stoeber's death, people in his home town started working on the ball of twine again. They gather each August in the city of Cawker for a twine-a-thon which includes a parade and town picnic. You'll be glad to know that because of their passion for Frank's project, Cawker City, Kansas is no longer home to the World's Second Largest Ball of Twine, but is now home to the World's Largest.

That's the power of passion.

SERVICE

Jesus knew that the Father had put all things under his power … so he got up from the meal, took off his outer clothing, and wrapped a towel around his waist. After that, he poured water into a basin and began to wash his disciples' feet.

—John 13:3–5

The scene was so powerful that I can still recall every detail even though it happened almost twenty years ago.

Linda had an important job. She was the bell ringer for the Lake Aurora Christian Camp. Time to wake up—Linda rang the bell. Time for chapel—Linda rang the bell. Time to clean up for dinner … you get the idea. Linda was good at her job. She knew people were counting on her so she faithfully served. I can't remember a time during all my weeks of camp that Linda ever forgot to ring the bell. She was a good bell ringer, a great person, and a true servant.

Linda was born with some physical and mental challenges that made her extra special to those who knew her. We all loved her and grew accustomed to her slurred speech, slow walk, loud laugh, and child-like personality. Her disabilities prevented her from working, but she refused to let them prevent her from serving. For about a decade, Linda served each camp director and camper faithfully by ringing the bell whenever it was needed.

One muggy Friday night in the summer of 1985, we were gathered in the chapel for a special service. All of the lights in the room were out except for one flickering fluorescent bulb directly above the stage. The windows were open (air-conditioning at camp is for wimps), and we could hear the rain falling outside. Ron, our camp director, walked on stage and read from John 13. He then set his Bible down, picked up a towel and basin, and began to wash the feet of his camp staff members. We watched in silence as Ron washed the feet of our counselors, teachers, cooks, and lifeguards and told them how much he loved them. Ron was a legend, and his weeks of camp were popular, so the chapel was packed with campers. We all loved and respected Ron, so we were not completely comfortable watching our leader wash feet.

I'm not sure how long the service was, but I know how it ended. We thought Ron was done, but then he unexpectedly asked the bell ringer to come up front. Linda took her seat and Ron began to wash her feet. She seemed very uncomfortable. Linda had spent most of her life being invisible. Her disabilities provided her a cloak which permitted her to serve without ever really having to be noticed. Now she was sitting on a stage being served, and she was overcome with emotion. We were all overcome with emotion. Linda cried, Ron cried, and a room full of teenagers cried as we all thought about Jesus. I'll never forget what I felt watching Ron wash Linda's feet, and I'll never forget what I learned about service from that dedicated director.

John 13 opens in the upper room. This event was so significant that every detail was apparently seared into John's mind. It was Thursday, and within twenty-four hours Jesus would be dead. It was time. He knew it, but his disciples still didn't. As John reflected back on that last night with Jesus, he made a point of recording what Christ knew:

"Jesus *knew* that the time had come for him to leave this world and go to the Father" (John 13:1).

"Jesus *knew* that the Father had put all things under his power, and that he had come from God and was returning to God" (John 13:3).

"For he *knew* who was going to betray him" (John 13:11).

Jesus knew what was about to happen, and he desperately wanted his disciples to know and understand why he came, why he lived, and why he was going to die. He wanted them to know that his entire existence was about others.

He created this world for us. He ordained the Law for us. He called out prophets for us. He sent himself for us. He ministered for us. He healed for us. He suffered for us. He died for us. He is creating heaven for us.

For us! God has done so much for us and all he wants is for us to return the favor and serve the people who share this world with us. Who do we think we are? Who do we think other people are?

Jesus knew who he was ...

"Jesus knew that the Father had put all things under his power" (John 13:3). I feel pretty powerful when I'm holding a TV remote control. God gave Jesus the power to turn the sun on and off. Jesus had the power to stop the earth from rotating. Jesus even had the power to make cows fly.

Jesus knew that "he had come from God" (John 13:3). I'm from Ohio. I'm a Buckeye, but that doesn't make my life any better. Jesus is from God. He was there before *there* was there. He was here before *here* was here. He's friends with angels. He can see yesterday and tomorrow at the same time. He can listen to and answer millions of prayers every second of every day for all eternity.

Jesus knew that he "was returning to God" (John 13:3). I'm going to North Carolina next week.... *Wow.* Jesus was about to go to heaven! Jesus was about to sit at the right hand of God. He was about to go to his "Father's House" and build mansions out of gold for us (John 14:2).

So ... knowing all of this about himself, he did what any of us would have done with all of the power of the universe at our disposal. He washed toe jam and fish guts out from between his disciples' toes to show them—and us—"the full extent of his love" (John 13:1).

Foot washing was a nice thing to do to honor your guests. Roads in the Near East were dusty and dirty and people wore sandals, so it was an act of hospitality to offer guests water to wash their feet. It was a sign of special welcome and devotion when the host did the washing. A host would customarily provide water for his guests upon their arrival, but foot washing typically was done by the lowliest servant, since it was considered the most menial task a servant could perform. So, Peter was completely justified in not believing what he was seeing, "Lord, are you going to wash my feet?" (John 13:6). Peter knew what we know: feet are gross and God is not. Peter couldn't allow Jesus to do this. "'No,' said Peter, 'you shall never wash my feet.' Jesus answered, 'Unless I wash you, you have no part with me'" (John 13:8).

To which Peter replied, "Okay, then. Give me a sponge bath!"[1]

The disciples were shocked, but they shouldn't have been. Jesus was doing what he had been doing since before time began and was doing what he expects us to do. Jesus asked a question he already knew the answer to, "Do you understand what I have done for you?" (John 13:12). Of course they didn't, and of course we struggle with it, too.

Jesus came to serve. Mark wrote, "For even the Son of Man did not come to be served, but to serve" (Mark 10:45). Jesus hoped that we would follow his example. He said, "You call me 'Teacher' and 'Lord,' and rightly so, for that is what I am. Now that I, your Lord and Teacher, have washed your feet, you also should wash one another's feet. I have set you an example that you should do as I have done for you" (John 13:13–15).

The disciples' feet were dirty, but this event is not about dirty feet; it's about proud hearts. It's about Christ-followers who refuse to follow Christ and serve.

Our answer to Christ's question can change this world: "Do you understand what I have done for you?"

Recently, I read about some church planters in China who demonstrated that they understood what Jesus was trying to teach. They thought they'd failed miserably. Sixteen Chinese Christians went to a rural area to plant churches but got absolutely no response from the people. They were destitute, living in the forest, and scavenging just enough food to keep them alive. Discouraged, they fasted for a week and prayed for God's guidance. When they gathered to discuss what they should do, each person said that God was saying to stay and "wash their feet."

For three years, they sat on the side of the road with buckets of water offering to wash the farmers' feet as they were coming and going from the fields. The offer annoyed the farmers, who regularly beat the evangelists and poured their water over them. But the Christians didn't give up. Finally, one of the farmers let one of the Christians wash his feet, and when he did, the other farmers relented. For three months, they washed 1,500 farmers' feet twice a day, until one of the farmers asked, "Why are you doing this?" Three years and three months after they decided to stay and wash feet, they finally got to proclaim the gospel. A few weeks later, the gospel had triumphed in the hearts of the farmers and they all placed their faith in Jesus Christ, as did another 50,000 residents of the region within the following two years.[2]

At the end of this event Jesus said, "Now that you *know* these things, you will be blessed if you do them" (John 13:17). You and I will have a more abundant life if only we will serve. If we begin to live as if we understand what Christ has done for us, then we will not hesitate to serve anyone, anywhere, at any time, and this world will be changed.

Every single mom will have a free babysitter while she attends night school.

Every latchkey kid will have a mentor to hang out with after school.

Every nursing home resident will have regular visitors.

Every widow will have clean gutters.

Every Sunday school class at your church will have a teacher.

Every recovering alcoholic will have a ride to work.

Every yard of every shut-in will be cut and edged regularly.

Every nursery shift at every church will be fully staffed.

Every child with AIDS will have someone to read to him or her before nap time.

Every dying person will have loving company and won't be alone in his or her last days.

Every orphan will have a mommy and a daddy.

Every lonely person will eat with someone else at least once a week.

Every lost person will have a friend who knows Jesus.

And every bell ringer will get her feet washed at least once in her life.

If we truly understand Jesus, then we will be changed and this world will be changed.

That's what's so ironic about service. When we serve, we give ... but we also get.

Refuel!

1. Contact the activities director at a local nursing home to set up a visit.

2. Spend an afternoon visiting with the residents.

3. What did you learn about the residents?

4. What did you learn about yourself?

5. Why not consider visiting the nursing home on a regular basis?

Focus

And if I go and prepare a place for you, I will come back and take you
to be with me that you also may be where I am.

—*John 14:3*

There are 530 identifiable phobias today.[1] Here are some of my favorites:

Ecclesiophobia—Fear of church.
Chronophobia—Fear of time.
Dutchphobia—Fear of the Dutch.
Phagophobia—Fear of being eaten.
Coulrophobia—Fear of clowns.
Ranidaphobia—Fear of frogs.
Ailurophobia—Fear of cats.
Homilophobia—Fear of sermons.
Gatorfanophobia—Fear of Florida Gator Fans (OK, I made this one up. Go 'Noles!).

The most common fear is Thanatophobia—Fear of death.

It has been claimed that one can never look directly at the sun or at one's own death. People don't like to think about dying. The fear of death is a universal phenomenon. Woody Allen once said, "I'm not afraid to die, I just don't want to be there when it happens." I have some bad news for Woody: unless Christ returns in our lifetime, death is an unavoidable appointment we'll all have to keep.

No matter where you go in the world, you will always find large numbers of people who are afraid of dying. The reason is obvious: death stinks. I've felt that way since early in my life. One day when I was in kindergarten, our field trip was to walk across the street to my house and see our guinea pig and her new babies. This was in the days before permission slips, "danger strangers," and—obviously—good field trips. This was potentially a great day for me. I knew that this day could make me popular and secure my identity as the coolest kid in kindergarten.

When we arrived at my house, Mom led us all downstairs to see the wonder of new life. Our joyful anticipation and giggling turned into grief and tears as we discovered a cage full of death. We were all horrified to discover that sometime in the night, my guinea pig and all her babies died. Any chance I had of ever being popular died with them.

That will leave a mark.

Death stinks. Our Father agrees with me about that. God hates death so much that he sent Jesus to this planet to defeat it. He definitely doesn't want us to be thanatophobic.

John 14 begins with Jesus and the twelve disciples still in the upper room. In this room, Jesus was carefully preparing his friends for his death. While they were eating, he picked up a piece of bread and broke it. He gave it to his disciples and told them that it was his body and he wanted them to remember that every time they ate it. He then picked up a cup of wine and told his disciples to drink it and remember that it was his blood that was shed for them. After this, he told them that he would be with them only a little while longer. This was not new information; he'd been talking about laying down his life since the beginning of his ministry. But something about this was different. It seemed more urgent—as if something terrible were about to happen. His disciples were starting to be gripped by fear. Jesus knew that unless he prepared them, their experiences in the next twenty-four hours might overwhelm them. Jesus didn't want them to be overcome by the fear of death, so he said, "Do not let your hearts be troubled. Trust in God; trust also in me" (John 14:1).

Has your heart ever been troubled?

When my dad died of a massive heart attack on August 8, 1988, my heart was troubled. My dad had been preaching in Ohio when he died. I was nineteen and working for the summer in Yellowstone National Park in Wyoming, and my mom was at home in Orlando, Florida, when I received the phone call.

Before I boarded the plane to fly back to Florida for my dad's funeral, I called home. Our dear family friend and one of my mentors, Dr. Paul Johnson, answered the phone. I was troubled and was becoming overwhelmed by grief. Doc Johnson could sense that I needed help making it home, so he said, "Son, your mother needs you to be strong. This is where the rubber meets the road. Come home quickly. I'll see you when you get here."

His words sustained me because they focused me. I was becoming overwhelmed as I thought about the future without my dad. I thought about the things he would miss: my college graduation, my wedding, the birth of my children, and long talks about raising kids over a morning cup of coffee. I began to grieve the loss of the future, and I was feeling overwhelmed because I was "worrying about tomorrow" (see Matt. 6:34). Dr. Johnson's words helped me to focus. I was in shock and grieving, but I didn't feel so overwhelmed after speaking to him, because I realized that the first thing I needed to do was get home. As I boarded that plane in Bozeman, Montana, I was okay. My heart had been focused on home.

Coach O'Brien, my track coach, taught me some important things. He was full of wisdom. One of the most valuable lessons he taught me had little to do with track and a lot to do with life.

I ran the 440, the 880, and the mile, and in the longer races, I had a recurring problem of drifting at the end. I would grow tired, drift out of my lane, slow down, and not reach the finish line as quickly. He said, "You'll reach what you're looking at." So he focused my attention on a big oak tree that stood just beyond the finish line. He said, "Look at that tree. Focus on it. Run toward it, and you'll stay in your lane and maybe even win."

The tree was there long before the track was even a dream. It sometimes seemed that that tree was timeless. I can't tell you how many races it delivered me through. It was always there, and focusing on it brought me home.

In the upper room, Jesus focused the disciples' troubled hearts on home.

Homes have always been important. The disciples understood the importance of housing. The houses they knew were simplistic. They were constructed out of mud-dried bricks and loose stones and had roofs made of pieces of wood. Most homes had floors made of clay since wood was too precious to be wasted on flooring. Simple windows were most often just an opening in the wall. Housing was designed to be practical. In Palestine, life consisted primarily of outdoor activities, so houses were used chiefly for sleeping and storage—not for living.

There were no thirty-year mortgages in Palestine.

So, the idea of a mansion in heaven would have been an amazing and wonderful concept. It would have been something worth living for. Jesus wanted his disciples to have something to focus on, because the events of the next few days might tempt them to drift off course. He wanted them to make it home.

Likewise, Jesus wants us to have something to focus on, because the events of our lives might tempt us to drift off course. He wants us to make it home to heaven, so he gave us (and his disciples) several important reasons why we should focus on heaven when our hearts are troubled.

First he said, "In my *Father's* house" (John 14:2), which reminds us that we have a Father in heaven. A lot of people are living in homes without a father. One of my best friends growing up had a rough home life. I called him my patriotic friend because he had "four fathers." For this reason, he gravitated toward my dad who in turn loved him like his own son. Despite what some modern experts think, it seems that studies are showing that kids need dads.

According to a report published in the *Washington Times*:[2]

- From 1960 to 1996, the number of children who lived in homes without a father or stepfather rose steadily—from 7 million to 20 million.
- Thirty-four percent of children live in homes without their biological father.

When we get to heaven everyone will have a father.

Second, Jesus said, "In my Father's house are *many* rooms; if it were not so, I would have told you. I am going there to prepare *a place for you*. And if I go and prepare *a place for you* ..." (John 14:2–3), which tells us that we should focus on heaven because we will have a place in heaven. There is a place being prepared just for you and me. I can't remember a time when I've had my own room. In heaven, Jesus is preparing a place big enough for you, me, and the millions of others who have put their hope and faith in him.

In Revelation 21 and 22 we read an incredible description of what our heavenly home will be like. Based on Revelation 21:15–21, here's what we know about our heavenly home:

- It will be as long as it is wide. The walls will be 216 feet wide. It will be 1,500 miles around—375 miles on each side. You won't be able to see the top with the naked eye.
- If the city were divided into rooms measuring a quarter mile each way, there would be room for 3,375,000,000 rooms.
- If we began to visit those rooms spending one hour in each room for twenty-four hours a day, at the end of 6,000 years we would have visited 52,570,560 rooms and have

3,322,529,440 rooms to go. It would take over 385,000 years to visit every room in New Jerusalem.

And that's just the city! We have a big, beautiful home waiting for us. This hope must focus our troubled hearts.

Third, Jesus said, "And if I go and prepare a place for you, I will come back and take you to be *with me that you also may be where I am*" (John 14:3), which tells us that we will not be alone in heaven. Jesus doesn't want us to ever think that we are alone. One of the last things he said to his disciples was, "And surely I am with you always, to the very end of the age" (Matt. 28:20). Loneliness breeds fear, and fear distracts us from the hope we have in Christ. Christ's disciples needed to know that despite how brutally Christ was going to be ripped out of their midst, he would not be gone for long or forever.

Kids often suffer from separation anxiety. We own a children's video that contains a song written to help kids who are afraid of being left alone:

Your mommy comes back.
She always comes back.
She always comes back to get you.
Your mommy comes back.
She always comes back.
She never will forget you.[3]

I often sang this song to my kids when their mommy had to leave and their hearts were beginning to become troubled. Jesus sang a similar song to his children. "I will come back and take you to be with me that you may also be where I am." He wanted them to know that they wouldn't be alone, so that they could focus on making it home.

There is more to this life. There is a goal worth reaching, and when we focus on that goal, we will make it home. Sometimes, though, we may need someone like my track coach to help us find that focus.

David Bigoney is a winner. He has focused his heart and life on victory. That focus is inspirational. I compete in triathlons. In May of 2002, David and I raced in a Half-Ironman distance race in Panama City, Florida. I saw David throughout the day: I saw him come out of the water after the 1.2-mile ocean swim, I saw him halfway through his 56-mile bike ride, and I was there when he crossed the finish line after running 13.1 miles. David is an amazing athlete, is intensely focused, and is a truly inspirational person. There's more to the story, though.

REFUEL!

1. Take time out to watch The Wizard of Oz.

2. What did Dorothy endure during her mission to make it home?

3. What are you willing to do to make it to your heavenly home?

In 1996, David was involved in a shooting which left him completely blind. In March 2001, at the age of 29, David embarked on a new stage in his life—the challenge of triathlons. David competes in a category for the physically challenged, which involves the use of a sighted guide in all three events (swimming, cycling, and running). In 2002, David competed in the World Triathlon Championships as the only blind male triathlete on Team USA.

However, David can't finish the race without a friend. This friend must swim 1.2 miles tied to David, ride tandem with David for 56 miles, and then run 13.1 miles tied to and guiding his blind friend.

David's friend is also an amazing and inspirational person.

David's friend encourages him, guides him, and constantly focuses him toward the finish line. David puts his trust in his friend to lead him where he can't go by himself, and he reaches his destination

Put your trust in your trusted friend. Let him focus your troubled heart on home and take you to a place you can't go by yourself. Suddenly, you'll find yourself making it home.

FRUIT

If a man remains in me and I in him, he will bear much fruit.

—*John 15:5*

Irecently heard that the last orange groves on the fifty-mile long Orange Blossom Trail here in Orlando have been cut down. I'm not that old, but back in my day if you were riding down OBT, you could see groves that looked like they stretched on forever. Now there's not one grove left standing beside that road. That's kind of sad, but it happens.

Truth be told, many of those trees were dead or dying anyway and hadn't borne substantial fruit in years. No fruit, no money; no money, no sense keeping the trees. The purpose of orange trees is oranges, and when they no longer bear fruit, they are useless.

Jesus doesn't want our lives to be useless or fruitless. Fruitful Christians were a part of Christ's plan even before he began his ministry. Before Christ's baptism, John the Baptizer proclaimed, "The ax is already at the root of the trees, and every tree that does not produce good fruit will be cut down and thrown into the fire" (Matt. 3:10). In the first sermon of his ministry Jesus said, "Every tree that does not bear good fruit is cut down and thrown into the fire" (Matt. 7:19). Trees that do not produce fruit are thrown into the fire. Isn't that harsh? Where's the patience? Couldn't the fruit tree be given a second chance? Where's the love for the poor, unproductive little fruit tree that was probably neglected as a sprout?

Jesus created trees to bear fruit and when they don't ... well ... check this out.

Early one morning during the last week of his life, Jesus was walking back to Jerusalem from Bethany and he was hungry. Jesus loved to use illustrations from nature in his sermons: birds of the air, lilies of the field, salt of the earth—you get the idea. Just a few days before his crucifixion, Jesus used a tree as—to quote the teens in my youth group—the "mack-daddy" of all nature props. Matthew told us what happened. "Seeing a fig tree by the road, he went up to it but found nothing on it except leaves. Then he said to it, 'May you never bear fruit again!' Immediately the tree withered. When the disciples saw this, they were amazed" (Matt. 21:19–20).

Awesome!

I wish I could make things wither with words. I would love to be able to simply speak and watch all of the weeds in my yard wither away, the thorns on the rose bushes dry up and fall off, and the cat next door ... sorry ... I got a little carried away.

Jesus spoke to a fruitless tree, and it shriveled up. This image of a withered fig tree had to flash back into the minds of the disciples when just a few days later Jesus said, "I am the true vine, and my Father is the gardener. He cuts off every branch in me that bears no fruit ... This is to my Father's glory, that you bear much fruit ... You did not choose me, but I chose you and appointed you to go and bear fruit—fruit that will last" (John 15:1–2, 8, 16).

The disciples had a job to do, and Jesus wanted them to do it. Jesus created us to bear fruit; not to bear fruit is to disobey our Creator. In this passage we see two things that must happen in order for us to bear fruit.

First, we must be pruned. Jesus said, "He cuts off every branch in me that bears no fruit, while every branch that does bear fruit he prunes so that it will be even more fruitful" (John 15:2–3). Pruning is unpleasant but essential if fruit production is the goal. Pruning is the process of cutting back and cutting off. In his commentary on the gospel of John, Merrill Tenney describes the pruning process:

> In pruning a vine, two principles are generally observed: first, all dead wood must be ruthlessly removed; and second, the live wood must be cut back drastically. Dead wood harbors insects and disease and may cause the vine to rot, to say nothing of being unproductive and unsightly. Live wood must be trimmed back in order to prevent such heavy growth that the life of the vine goes into the wood rather than into fruit. The vineyards in the early spring look like a collection of barren, bleeding stumps; but in the fall they are filled with luxuriant purple grapes ... from those who have suffered the most there often comes the greatest fruitfulness.[1]

God prunes us so that we will be more fruitful.

How is God pruning you? Is he cutting back your self-confidence so you have more God-confidence? Is he cutting off your pride so that you'll be more like Jesus? Is he cutting back your income so that you'll serve him rather than serving money? Is he cutting off your comfort zone so that you'll go where he wants you to go?

Pruning occurs for our benefit, whether we think we need it or not. Job was faithfully serving God. Job "was blameless and upright; he feared God and shunned evil" (Job 1:1). Why did he need to be pruned? God allowed Satan to prune everything from Job because he knew Job could handle it. God also permitted it because he knew we would need Job's example. We needed Job in order to know that it can always be worse, and it can always be endured—with God. In Job we read, "Blessed is the man whom God corrects; so do not despise the discipline of the Almighty. For he wounds, but he also binds up; he injures, but his hands also heal" (Job 5:17–18).

God prunes us to make us stronger, better, and more mature. I draw encouragement from what I read in Hebrews:

> "My son, do not make light of the Lord's discipline, and do not lose heart when he rebukes you, because the Lord disciplines those he loves, and he punishes everyone he accepts as a son" ... but God disciplines us for our good, that we may share in his holiness. No discipline seems pleasant at the time, but painful. Later on, however, it produces a harvest of righteousness and peace for those who have been trained by it. (Heb. 12:5–6, 10–11)

God sustains me also through the words from James, the brother of Jesus:

> Consider it pure joy, my brothers, whenever you face trials of many kinds, because you know that the testing of your faith develops perseverance. Perseverance must finish its work so that you may be mature and complete, not lacking anything. (James 1:2–4)

Pruning precedes fruit. Remember the fruit when you are facing the trial. God is not going to waste any of your pain.

The second thing that must happen in order for us to bear fruit is that we must be connected to the tree. Jesus said, "No branch can bear fruit by itself; it must remain in the vine. Neither can you bear fruit unless you remain in me. I am the vine; you are the branches. If a man remains in me and I in him, he will bear much fruit; apart from me you can do nothing" (John 15:4–5). If we want to bear fruit then we must be connected to Jesus. Disciples who are connected to Jesus are powerful; disciples who are independent of Jesus are pitiful. Jesus wants his disciples to know that they need him and will die if they try to minister without him.

Are you connected to Jesus? More importantly, are you bearing fruit?

We can go to church, read our Bible, and pray sixty-three times a day, but if we are not sharing Christ with lost people, using our spiritual gifts for God's glory, serving the needs of the poor, sick, orphans, and widows, and living a life that honors Christ completely, then we are not bearing fruit. And the only way to bear true spiritual fruit is to be connected to Christ.

REFUEL!

1. Buy a small house plant. Tear off a branch from the houseplant and lay it beside the plant.
2. Read John 15.
3. Set the plant and the branch in a place where you can see it each day.
4. Once the branch dies—and it will die—put it in your wallet or purse as a constant reminder to stay connected to Jesus.

Last Christmas I was reminded once again of the importance of being connected to Christ. I love Christmas. Christmas is a magical time full of wonderful traditions. One of our traditions is to cut our own Christmas tree. We used to buy our trees in a parking lot because we live in Florida and we thought that was our only option. Then, we found a Christmas tree farm only an hour away from our house. My earliest memories of Christmas in Ohio include trudging through the cold and snow searching for the perfect tree. When we found the perfect tree, Dad would cut it down and we would drag it to the car. I was so excited to begin this tradition anew with my family.

We cut down the live tree, take it home, and water it like crazy. That's my job: lie on my back and pour water into that tiny little tree holder hoping not to get the presents all wet. As Christmas draws near, the tree drinks less and less water, until finally it stops drinking altogether. My goal each year is to keep the tree alive just long enough for Christmas morning. If the tree dies on the day after Christmas ... perfect.

One morning this Christmas season I had an epiphany as I lay on my back reaching my arm through the needles trying to water the tree. I realized that a live Christmas tree is not really a live Christmas tree at all. My "live" Christmas tree began to die the moment it was cut off from its roots. Once my tree was cut off from the nourishment of its root system, its fate was secure. We can dress it up and put lights on it, but it's really only delaying the inevitable. The only way for a live Christmas tree to really be considered "live" is for it to remain attached to its roots.

Are you really alive? There's a famous quote by well-known journalist and novelist Norman Mailer that I like: "Every moment of one's existence one is growing into more or retreating into less. One is always living a little more or dying a little bit." We may be beautifully decorated and admired by many as if we were something special, but unless you and I are directly connected to Jesus Christ then our fate is secure. We will not bear fruit without Jesus and we will not—we can not—really live without Jesus.

My church just bought some land off of Orange Blossom Trail that we're going to use to construct our new church building. Yesterday I found a spot out by the road in which I'm going to plant a new tree to represent our commitment to the community. I think I'll plant an orange tree.

PEACE

I have told you these things, so that in me you may have peace.

—John 16:33

A former president of the Norwegian Academy of Sciences and a group of historians from England, Egypt, Germany, and India have come up with some startling information: since 3600 BC, the world has known only 292 years of peace! Outside those few peaceful times, there have been 14,351 wars, large and small, in which 3.64 billion people have been killed. The value of the property destroyed would pay for a golden belt around the world 97.2 miles wide and 33 feet thick. Since 650 BC, there have also been 1,656 arms races, only sixteen of which have not ended in war. The remainder ended in the economic collapse of the countries involved.[1]

Wouldn't it make more sense to learn how to get along?

We all face war in our personal lives. Some of us face war in our hearts and minds. Maybe you fight with stress and the pressures of living. Maybe your battle is against depression, and you fight daily for your survival.

Some of us face war in our homes. Maybe a place that should be safe and sound has become a place of torment. Broken vows, broken hearts, and broken dreams can turn families into enemies.

Some of us face war at our jobs. Maybe you have to fight

seemingly senseless battles with coworkers or with a boss in power struggles and back-biting. Maybe your work environment is so oppressive you think you might suffocate. Some of us face war in our souls. Maybe you don't feel peace with God. Maybe as you read this, you're not too sure you even believe in God because of all the problems you face.

Some look for peace in meditation, convinced that crossed legs, closed eyes, and silence will bring a cease-fire to the soul. Some look for peace by taking a vacation only to discover the problems waiting anxiously for them at home. Some look for peace in pleasure, disappointed to find that when the party's over, there's still a mess to clean up. Some look for peace in spending money, hoping that a new outfit, car, or home will finally purchase contentment for their troubled soul. Some look for peace in substances, trying to escape the pain through alcohol or drugs only to awake on the front line again.

The only way to find peace in our lives is to find the Prince of Peace. Jesus is all about peace.

About 700 years before Christ's birth, God gave Isaiah the promise that wars would end one day. Isaiah prophesied of Christ's birth and ministry when he said, "And he will be called Wonderful Counselor, Mighty God, Everlasting Father, Prince of Peace. Of the increase of his government and peace there will be no end" (Isa. 9:6–7). On the night of Christ's birth the angels proclaimed, "Glory to God in the highest, and on earth peace to men on whom his favor rests" (Luke 2:14). In his first sermon he taught peace, "Blessed are the peacemakers, for they will be called sons of God" (Matt. 5:9). On the night before his death as he left the upper room he encouraged his disciples with peace, "Peace I leave with you; my peace I give you. I do not give to you as the world gives. Do not let your hearts be troubled and do not be afraid" (John 14:27). And as he prepared for his crucifixion, he wished peace upon his friends: "I have told you these things, so that in me you may have peace. In this world you will have trouble. But take heart! I have overcome the world" (John 16:33).

And in this world we *do* have trouble. And though over 8,000 peace treaties have been broken throughout recorded history, I haven't given up hope. I long for peace in my life and in yours. Jesus longs for peace in our lives as well.

John 16 opens when Christ's arrest was only hours away. The drums of war were pounding, the betrayer had already betrayed his master, soldiers were beginning to gather, swords were being sharpened, and the enemies of Jesus were anticipating victory. The tension was high as Jesus continued to prepare his friends for the spiritual battle about to begin. He warned, "They will put you out of the synagogue; in fact, a time is coming when anyone who kills you will think he is offering a service to God" (John 16:2). He continued, "I have told you this, so that when the time comes you will remember that I warned you" (John 16:4). Jesus was preparing them for battle, but ironically the only weapon that he permitted his followers to use was peace. Peace is more powerful than any weapon, and Christ was counting on the power of peace to protect the hearts of his disciples as they watched his execution and fought the urge to fight back. Jesus told them three things intended to bring them peace.

First, He Told Them That Help Was on the Way.

Jesus said, "But I tell you the truth: It is for your good that I am going away. Unless I go away, the Counselor will not come to you; but if I go, I will send him to you" (John 16:7). The Holy Spirit had been around since page one of the Bible: "Now the earth was formless and empty, darkness was over the surface of the deep, and the Spirit of God was hovering over the waters" (Gen. 1:2). The Holy Spirit also came down at Christ's baptism, but Jesus told his disciples that the Holy Spirit wouldn't come again unless he went away.

And he wanted them to want the help of the Holy Spirit. The

Holy Spirit was going to be an amazing help and source of peace for them. Earlier in the evening Jesus said, "the Counselor, the Holy Spirit, whom the Father will send in my name, will teach you all things and will remind you of everything I have said to you. *Peace I leave with you; my peace I give you....* Do not let your hearts be troubled and do not be afraid" (John 14:26–27). And then he taught them that when the Holy Spirit would finally come, the Spirit would help them by making sure that their message was powerful and would convict people of the guilt of their sin (see John 16:8–11) and would make their preaching truthful (see John 16:13–15).

What a blessing! These ordinary men were facing an extraordinary job without the physical presence of their leader so they needed the help of the Holy Spirit. The Holy Spirit would teach them, help them remember everything Jesus said, empower their message, and make sure that everything they said was true. They would have peace because they would have help.

We have help, too. In Christ we are not alone. We have the indwelling and empowering gift of the presence of the person of the Holy Spirit working in our lives.

The Holy Spirit is ...

A person to be listened to—Acts 13:2

A person who works for us—1 Corinthians 12:11

An intelligent person—Isaiah 11:2

A loving helper—2 Timothy 1:14

The Holy Spirit is an incredible resource for us who ...

Thinks—Romans 8:27

Knows—1 Corinthians 2:10–11

Directs—Acts 16:7

Speaks—Acts 13:2

Loves—Romans 15:30

Helps—Romans 8:26

And we must be so careful to respect the Holy Spirit, because the Holy Spirit ...

Can be lied to—Acts 5:3

Can be tested—Acts 5:9

Can be resisted—Acts 7:51

Can be grieved—Ephesians 4:30

He is our help and a source of peace.

SECOND, JESUS TOLD THEM THAT POWER WAS ON THE WAY.

Jesus said, "In that day you will no longer ask me anything. I tell you the truth, my Father will give you whatever you ask in my name.... Ask and you will receive" (John 16:23–24). The disciples needed this special promise of special power for their special ministry. When they began their ministry, they had no written gospel or letters to the churches, and no proof that Jesus was who he said he was other than their testimony to the miracles and resurrection. They needed God to give them the resources for telling people about Jesus and convincing them that he really was the son of God.

God keeps his promises. So, about fifty days after the resurrection, during the feast of Pentecost, the original eleven apostles (Judas was dead) along with Matthias, the newest apostle, were gathered together when God's power showed up—just as promised—through the Holy Spirit. The power of God came upon them, and these Galilean men were given the ability to speak foreign languages, but that was just the beginning. Luke recorded that as the apostles began their ministry, "Everyone was filled with awe, and many wonders and miraculous signs were done by the apostles" (Acts 2:43). The disciples knew that they weren't going to have to depend on their own power, so they could be at peace, even in the presence of a daunting task.

We can have peace too, because we also have access to the power of God. Later in his ministry John wrote, "This is the confidence we have in approaching God: that if we ask anything according to his will, he hears us. And if we know that he hears us—whatever we ask—we know that we have what we asked of him" (1 John 5:14–15). When we go to God in the midst of battle and ask for his help, seeking his will, then we can be confident, knowing that he has heard us and will do what is best for us. We should ask humbly, yet confidently expect more because God is powerful.

Let's ask God for more—more than we see, more than we know.

Charles F. Kettering recalls how he encouraged his employees to ask for more. "When I was research head of General Motors and wanted a problem solved, I'd place a table outside the meeting room with a sign: *Leave slide rules here.* If I didn't do that, I'd find someone reaching for his slide rule. Then he'd be on his feet saying, 'Boss, you can't do it.'"[2] So often it seems we don't ask for a display of God's power because we're convinced that "He can't do it." He can! And he *will* if we'll ask.

THIRD, JESUS TOLD THEM THAT VICTORY WAS ON THE WAY.

Jesus said, "I have told you these things, so that in me you may have peace. In this world you will have trouble. But take heart! I have overcome the world" (John 16:33). The disciples were going to feel defeated. Jesus' arrest, trials, beatings, crucifixion, and death were not going to make the disciples feel like they were on the winning side. Satan would do all he could to make them lose heart.

Satan tried to intimidate the apostles, but he failed. They all served faithfully until their death, and most of them died as martyrs. Satan tries to intimidate us, too, but we must remember that we have already won the game and—no matter how many times he attacks us—we need not give in, give out, or give up because our God is more powerful than he is. We are on Christ's side and he never quits, always survives, always rises, always wins, and always comes back.

In the book *The Business of Heaven*, a collection of daily readings based on the writings of C. S. Lewis, we find the following encouragement from the wise theologian: "The moment you wake up each morning, all your wishes and hopes for the day rush at you like wild animals. And the first job each morning consists in shoving it all back; in listening to that other voice, taking that other point of view, letting that other, larger, stronger, quieter life come flowing in." The "other voice" we must listen to each day is the voice of Christ saying, "I have told you these things so that in me you may have peace." Each day give your battles to the Prince of Peace believing that help, power, and victory are on the way, and an abundant life will come flowing in to bring an end to the war of your soul.

 ## REFUEL!

1. As you read in this chapter, over 8,000 peace treaties have been entered into and broken over the years, but I still think we could try one more. You're going to enter into a peace treaty with God. Get a clean piece of paper, a pen, and a candle, and write the following:

GET A LIFE PEACE TREATY
(PRAY THIS AND THEN SIGN.)

LORD, TODAY I LAY DOWN MY WEAPONS AND
    SURRENDER TO YOU.
I TRUST YOU AND KNOW THAT YOU ARE ON MY SIDE.
I KNOW THAT YOU HAVE SENT THE HOLY SPIRIT TO
    HELP ME.
I KNOW THAT IF I ASK YOU FOR ANYTHING
    ACCORDING TO YOUR WILL, YOU WILL HEAR ME.

I KNOW THAT YOU HAVE OVERCOME THE WORLD.
YOUR ARE MY PRINCE OF PEACE,
AND TODAY I PROMISE TO STRIVE TO LIVE YOUR
PEACE EVERY DAY OF MY LIFE.

SIGNATURE: _____

DATE: _____

2. Now fold the treaty and seal it with wax from the candle. Keep this peace treaty as a reminder of the peace that Jesus wants for your life.

ℙRAYER

After Jesus said this, he looked toward heaven and prayed.

—John 17:1

ℙrayer is powerful.

I was reminded of that truth just a few weeks ago. I stayed late after Wednesday night Bible study for our bi-monthly leadership meeting at church. By the time I got home, it was after 11:00 p.m., and Rhonda and the kids were already asleep.

About 6:08 the next morning, my four-year-old son, Levi, crawled into bed with us. He likes to get up early, stand quietly at our bedside, and stare at us until we wake up and ask the all-important question, "Are you ready for a bowl of cereal?" But this morning he was content to let us lie in bed for a little while longer so he could lie there, too.

I was lying there chatting in soft whispers to my son when I said, "Levi, how 'bout you and I go fishing?"

"Now?" he replied joyfully. He bounded out of bed as he yelled, "Sure, I'll get my clothes on." As Levi and I quietly prepared to go, my wife—who's not a morning person, so she doesn't typically speak in the mornings until at least 10:00—started to say something. She spoke! It was an E. F. Hutton moment.

In a soft whisper she said, "Arron, last night as Levi was going to bed, he prayed that you would take him fishing when you woke up this morning."

Our God is amazing. With all of the stuff he has to deal with in the world, he still has time to make sure a four-year-old boy gets to go fishing with his dad. Isn't that cool?

Prayer is powerful.

According to the *Wordsmyth Educational Dictionary*, "Prayer is the act of appealing to and invoking the power of God or some spiritual being." Even this secular dictionary acknowledges that prayer is powerful ("invoking the power of God").

 REFUEL!

1. Watch the classic movie It's a Wonderful Life, *starring Jimmy Stewart.*

2. How did George Bailey's prayer change his life?

3. Have you ever had a prayer change your life? If so, in what ways did it make a difference?

The power of prayer recently has been debated, even outside of theological circles, because of some major studies. On August 13, 2001, the ABC news show "Downtown" aired a story about the power of prayer entitled "Can Prayer Heal?" In this segment, they reported that the National Institute of Health conducted a study and found that prayer is powerful. In the study, Dr. Elizabeth Targ, a psychiatrist at the Pacific College of Medicine in San Francisco, tested prayer on critically ill AIDS patients. All twenty patients in the study received the same medical treatment, but only half of them were prayed for. Ultimately, all ten of the prayed-for patients lived, while four who had not been prayed for died. In a larger follow-up study, Targ found that the people who received prayer had one-sixth the hospitalizations, and those hospitalizations were significantly shorter than the people who had not received prayer. "I was sort of shocked," said Targ. "In a way it's like witnessing a miracle. There was no way to understand this from my experience and from my basic understanding of science."[1]

Jesus didn't need a study; he already knew that prayer was powerful.

In John 17, which recounts the last night of his life, we are told an amazing thing. Jesus was talking to himself. Jesus is God—in the flesh—yet he's praying to God—not in the flesh. Now, if I talk to myself it's a little odd, but when Jesus talks to himself, it's inspirational. Jesus set such an amazing example for us by praying throughout his ministry. He prayed because prayer is powerful.

In his last moments of painless independence, Jesus prayed. He knew what was coming and could have run from it, but he kneeled instead. The almighty Creator of the universe prayed for himself, for his disciples, and for us. Why? Because prayer is powerful.

Do you believe in the power of prayer?

In his prayer for himself he prayed, "Father, the time has come. Glorify your Son, that your Son may glorify you" (John 17:1). Under the Old Testament system on the Day of Atonement, the High Priest would not do anything until he first purified himself. He needed to be right with God before helping others to become right with God. Jesus was as much man as he was God, and he didn't want his manhood to obscure his God-hood. Jesus wanted everyone who would watch him suffer and die to see God through it all.

In his prayer for his disciples he prayed, "My prayer is not that you take them out of the world but that you protect them from the evil one" (John 17:15). He loved these guys and didn't want them to be devoured by Satan. He knew what was going to happen to him, but he also knew what was going to happen to them. They had a job and it must be accomplished. Jesus didn't want them removed from the world, just Satan removed from theirs. God has the power to put hedges around us that will protect us from Satan (see Job 1:10). This was his prayer for his friends.

In his prayer for us he prayed, "I pray also for those who will believe in me through their message, that all of them may be one, Father, just as you are in me and I am in you" (John 17:20–21). As I look through the yellow pages under "Churches," I notice that there are about twenty pages of churches. I'm a minister in an independent Christian church. In my wife's hometown of about 15,000 people in the mountains of upper East Tennessee there are over thirty Christian churches alone. Churches compete with each other over territory, money, members, facilities, and softball. American Baptist, Lutheran, Free Methodist, Presbyterian Church in America, Presbyterian Church (U.S.A.), Church of God, Church of Christ, Pentecostal, Catholic, Episcopalian, Anglican, United Methodist, Wesleyan, Seventh Day Adventists, Free-Will Baptist, African Methodist Episcopal Church, International Church of Christ, Church of the Nazarene, Free Presbyterian, Southern Baptist Convention, Greek Orthodox, Christian & Missionary Alliance, Independent Christian Church ... Had enough? I know God has.

Our unity is much more important than the warm feeling we get when standing together in a circle holding hands and singing "Kum By Yah." Our unity is powerful. Christ shares two powerful results of our unity when he prayed, "May they be brought to complete unity to let the world know that you sent me and have loved them even as you have loved me" (John 17:23). Christ wanted us to be unified so that people would believe that Jesus was sent by God and believe that God loves them. That means that our disunity communicates that Jesus *was not* sent by God and that God *does not* love them. We must join Christ in praying for unity so that both Jesus and God's love will be easily recognized.

Prayer is powerful. Prayer makes us powerful. I've heard, "A prayer-less church is a powerless church." Well, I also believe that a prayer-less Christian is a powerless Christian. Jesus prayed because he needed the power of God to glorify him, protect his disciples, and unite us.

I've seen the power of prayer many times in my life, but one time stands out. My dad made his kids' sixteenth birthdays something special. My two older sisters and I were each officially recognized by my dad on our sixteenth birthdays as adults. The blessing I received on that day from my dad still sustains me today.

Dad died twenty-one days before my younger brother's sixteenth birthday. There are four kids in my family, and of us Adam had the strongest will. During the summer before Dad died, he and Adam butted heads again and again. Adam wanted to be a man, but was still making childish decisions. Dad was patiently and lovingly shaping and redirecting Adam's will into a blessing rather than a curse. Dad knew that he needed to redirect Adam's will, without breaking it.

In the days after Dad's death, Adam repeatedly said to my mom, "Dad won't ever see me as a man. His last memories will always be of me causing him trouble." Mom prayed.

As Adam's sixteenth birthday approached, he became more and more withdrawn and angry. Adam was going to have to live his entire life without "the blessing" of his father. Maybe you know how hard that is. Mom prayed that God would do something to resolve this issue in Adam's life.

My dad was a preacher and a Bible college professor when he died. The day before his funeral, Mom called down to the college campus and asked one of Dad's colleagues to look in his office files for an insurance document. Twila Sias, a teacher and family friend, searched in vain. Frustrated and grieving, she sat down in the quiet of my dad's office. In the midst of the hundreds of books in my dad's huge library, she noticed one book in particular—a book Dad had recently recommended.

Intrigued and grateful for the distraction, she glanced

through the book titled *Missing from Action: Vanishing Manhood in America.*[2] She read the inside jacket cover and then noticed that the book carried an inscription in Dad's handwriting—a gift of words prepared weeks in advance. She instantly recognized the significance of this book, drove the twenty-three miles to our family home, and handed the treasure to my mom.

Mom wrapped the book. Several days later on his sixteenth birthday, Adam opened the gift and read the message written by his father:

> *To Adam, on your 16th birthday,*
> *I like the man I see when I look at you.*
> *Love, Dad*

Mom's prayer was answered, and my brother's question was answered once and for all time.

Our God is amazing. With all of the stuff he has to deal with in the world, he still took time to make sure a sixteen-year-old boy received "the blessing" from his father. And he has time for you. Do you have time for him?

One night when my daughter was seven, she suggested a new prayer schedule to me and my wife: "I pray, you pray, and then Daddy prays ... until we die." It sounds like a good plan!

Friends, let's follow that plan for all the years of our lives here on earth: I pray and you pray ... until we die.

HOMESICKNESS

My kingdom is not of this world.

—John 18:36

On October 30, 1938, the United States experienced mass hysteria—particularly on the East Coast in New York and New Jersey—when Orson Welles and his *Mercury Theater on the Air* broadcast "War of the Worlds."

This broadcast of "War of the Worlds" was a fictional newscast of an invasion of earth by aliens, but the terror was real. People were horrified to think that aliens had invaded our planet. Little did they know that our planet was invaded by aliens a long time ago.

Christians are called "aliens" in this world, and early Christians felt like aliens (1 Peter 1:1, 17; 2:11). Early Christians were persecuted for their faith. At first the Roman authorities left Christians to themselves, but as the Christians refused to worship the many Roman gods and the emperor, persecution grew. The Christians were accused of false charges ranging from disloyalty to Rome to ritual cannibalism (the Lord's Supper). Christians were even held responsible for all natural calamities, such as plagues, floods, and famines.

In fact, the Christian religion was proclaimed by observers in the first centuries *"strana et illicita*—strange and unlawful" (Senatorial decree of the year 35), *"exitialis*—deadly" (Tacitus), "*prava et immodica*—wicked and unbridled" (Plinius), "*nova et malefica*—new and harmful" (Suetonius), "*tenebrosa et lucifuga*—mysterious and opposed to light" (from "Octavius" by Minucius), and "*detestabilis*—hateful" (Tacitus). Therefore, Christianity was outlawed, and Christians were persecuted because they were considered the most dangerous enemy of the power of Rome.

This persecution started with Jesus on the last night of his life. Christ entered Jerusalem to a hero's welcome. Palm branches and cloaks were strewn on the road to honor his arrival. The residents of this world praised him as their deliverer. He was one of their own, coming to deliver them from the hands of the Romans. They shouted, "Hosanna! Blessed is he who comes in the name of the Lord!" (John 12:13), but they were really saying, "Welcome Home!" The Jews thought that they were welcoming their king to his kingdom, but they did not understand that his kingdom was not of this world.

In John 18, we read that this world began to turn on Jesus. Judas turned on Jesus, betraying him with a kiss. The Jewish leaders turned on their Messiah, putting him through three trials (Annas, Caiaphas, and the Sanhedrin) and handing him over to the Romans. Peter, one of his own disciples, turned on him, denying knowing him three times. And the Romans turned on him, putting him through three more trials (Pilate, Herod, and Pilate again).

Has this world ever turned on you? It will.

As a young, innocent, and comfortable Christian I loved to sing the song, "This World is Not My Home." A great tune and catchy lyrics disguised a very serious message: we are aliens here.

I love life and so much of what it offers. I like my neighborhood. I like my house. I like watching *CSI*. I like the beach. Tennessee is a great place. I like Manhattan. Chick-Fil-A makes a great chicken sandwich. Ridgewood Bar-B-Q makes the best bleu-cheese dressing. *The Rookie* is a great movie. David

Letterman makes me laugh.... But as I watch the news and see wrong called right, as I hear of unborn children being aborted by the millions, as sin is celebrated in Hollywood, as God is mocked, as war spreads across the Middle East, as loving couples cry because they can't get pregnant, as churches split, as I watch ministers experience moral failure, as I do funerals of close friends, and as I visit my dad's grave, my soul cries out: "I can't feel at home in this world anymore!"

This world is an adulteress who mocks our affection and laughs while we cry.

You love your job, then out of nowhere you're fired and at risk of losing your house, and you don't feel at home here anymore. Your marriage was great, but then everything went bad and now, as you argue with your spouse over who will get the kids during the summer, you don't feel at home here anymore. You depended on your best friend and talked to her each day— you were as close as sisters—but you're both hurt and she won't return your phone calls, so you don't feel at home here anymore. You've always been healthy, but haven't felt too good for the past several months. Your doctor runs you through some tests and then tells you that he has some bad news for you, and you don't feel at home here anymore.

The older we get, the more life we experience and the less we feel at home here. I once heard someone say, "Trials break our allegiance to earth and turn our hearts toward heaven."

During Jesus' sixth and last trial, Pilate asked the question that ultimately got Christ killed, "Are you the king of the Jews?" (John 18:33). Jesus replied, "My kingdom is not of this world. If it were, my servants would fight to prevent my arrest by the Jews. But now my kingdom is from another place" (John 18:36). Pilate was having a close encounter with another kind. Jesus was not of this world and neither are his followers.

Is your kingdom of this world? Christians belong to a kingdom that is elsewhere, so we should feel a little strange or a little restless. We have a citizenship somewhere else. We are what Stanley Hauerwas and William Willimon call "Resident Aliens." In the preface to their book, they compare the kingdom of heaven to a colony. They write:

> A colony is a beachhead, an outpost, an island of one culture in the middle of another, a place where the values of home are reiterated and passed on to the young, a place where the distinctive language and life-style of the resident aliens are lovingly nurtured and reinforced ... in baptism our citizenship is transferred from one dominion to another, and we become, in whatever culture we find ourselves, resident aliens.[1]

An American tourist paid a visit to a renowned Polish rabbi, Hofetz Chaim. He was astonished to see that the rabbi's home was a simple room filled with nothing but books, a table, and a cot. The tourist asked the rabbi, "Where's all the furniture?"

"Where's yours?" the rabbi asked in return.

"Mine?" The tourist responded, "But I'm only visiting here. I'm only passing through."

To which the rabbi replied, "So am I."

We are just passing through. We're resident aliens who are only visiting here.

I can never really relax at someone else's house. People always say to their guests, "Make yourself at home." I always think, *You don't really mean that. Because if I can really make myself at home, then I'm putting on my favorite shorts (that used to be pants and now have huge oil stains on them from when I wore them to change the oil because it was Saturday morning and I didn't feel like putting real clothes on) and taking off my shoes and socks, drinking the orange juice out of the bottle, eating ice cream right out of the carton, tearing down your ugly drapes, getting in the middle of your argument, planting myself in the most comfortable chair in front of the TV, and grabbing the remote control with both hands.* That's what I do when I make myself at home—I get comfortable.

This world is not my home, though. I am a citizen of the kingdom of heaven. I'm only a resident alien whose mission is to get home and to take as many people as possible with me. We Christians are not supposed to be getting comfortable here. In fact, we're supposed to be uncomfortable here. As Jesus prepared his disciples for their lives on this planet he said, "If anyone would come after me, he must deny himself and take up his cross and follow me" (Matt. 16:24). It's impossible to get comfortable while carrying a cross.

We're going to feel persecuted.

We're going to feel strange.

We're not supposed to get their jokes.

We're not supposed to speak their language.

Their fights are not our fights.

Their home is not our home.

And I don't know about you, but I'm feeling a little homesick.

REFUEL!

1. Watch Apollo 13, *one of my favorite movies of all time.*

2. As their capsule passes around the dark side of the moon, Jim Lovell (Tom Hanks) notices that his crew is beginning to lose focus. He asks them a very important question: "Gentlemen, what are your intentions?" He then answers his own question. What is his answer? How does his answer change the focus of the mission?

3. I'd like you to answer the same question. You and I are on a mission. What are your intentions? I don't know about you, but I want to go home.

ELEMENT 19

VALUE

Jesus said, "It is finished." With that, he bowed his head and gave up his spirit.

—*John 19:30*

A couple of years ago we were preparing for our big Easter Sunday production. I was in my office reviewing the Easter video we were going to use in the service on Easter morning. I was so engrossed in the images of Christ being crucified that I didn't notice when my then two-year-old son Levi wandered into my office.

Absorbed in the video, I wasn't paying much attention to my son and the impact this video was having on him. It was a representation of the crucifixion of Jesus, and it was powerful. Levi pointed at Jesus and said, "Daddy ... he has owies." He repeated this several times before I recognized a teachable moment.

I stopped the tape and tried to explain to my son—as much as I thought a two-year-old could understand—the reason why Jesus was getting "owies."

His response was profound and unforgettable. He looked at me with a mystified look on his face and asked, "Daddy, Jesus get owies for me?" I began to cry. "Yes, Levi, Jesus got owies for you."

My friend, you are valuable; you are precious to God. No matter what you have come to believe about yourself you must know this one fact:

Even knowing your sin ...
Even knowing your imperfections ...
Even knowing your tendency toward self ...
Even knowing what you did when you were immature ...
Even knowing your misplaced affections ...
Jesus got owies for you and me.

John 19 tells of the beginning of the horror for Jesus, "Then Pilate took Jesus and had him flogged" (John 19:1). Eight words. No explanation or description of the horror of flogging. According to historians, about one-third of people who were flogged died while being flogged. In his book *A Ready Defense*, Josh McDowell describes flogging:

> The whip, known as a flagrum, had a sturdy handle to which were attached long leather thongs of varying lengths. Sharp, jagged pieces of bone and lead were woven into them. The Jews were limited by their law to 40 lashes. The Pharisees, with their emphasis on strict adherence to the law, would limit their lashes to 39, so that if they miscounted they would not break their law. The Romans had no such limitations. Out of disgust or anger, the Romans could totally ignore the Jewish limitation, and probably did so in the case of Jesus.[1]

Dr. C. Truman Davis, a medical doctor who meticulously studied crucifixion from a medical perspective, notes this about flogging:

> The heavy whip is brought down with full force again and again across (a person's) shoulders, back and legs. At first, the heavy thongs cut through cutaneous tissues, producing first an oozing of blood from the capillaries and veins of the skin, and finally spurting arterial bleeding from vessels in the underlying muscles. The small balls of lead first produce large, deep bruises which are broken open by subsequent blows. Finally the skin of the back is hanging in long ribbons and the entire area is an unrecognizable mass

of torn, bleeding tissue. When it is determined by the centurion in charge that the prisoner is near death, the beating is finally stopped.[2]

Eusebius, a historian from the third century, noted in *The Epistle of the Church in Symrna* that when someone was flogged, "The sufferer's veins were laid bare, and the very muscles, sinews, and bowels of the victim were open to exposure."[3]

I recently watched Mel Gibson's movie *The Passion of the Christ*. This movie was a powerful presentation of the suffering that Christ endured to redeem the world. I will never forget the scene which depicted Christ's flogging. For almost forty-five minutes I watched in silent horror as Christ's beating was vividly played out on the screen. I wanted to stand up and yell, "Stop it! He's had enough! Stop!" I prayed, "Lord, make me worthy of this." Jesus was flogged for you and for me.

REFUEL!

1. Watch Mel Gibson's The Passion of the Christ.
2. List the words that describe your feelings as you watched the movie.

After they flogged him, they put a crown of thorns on his head. Have you ever pricked your finger on a thorn from the stem of a rose given to you by someone who loves you? Hurts, doesn't it? Jesus had long thorns woven into a crown forced onto his head by professional executioners intent on mocking him.

Jesus wore a crown of thorns for you and for me.

They then put a purple robe on Jesus and began to mock him saying, "Hail, king of the Jews!" (John 19:3). As they mocked him, they struck his face. Have you ever been punched in the face?

Jesus was mocked and struck in the face for you and for me.

Pilate tried to set Jesus free saying to the Jews, "Here is your king" (John 19:14), but they shouted, "Take him away! Take him away! Crucify him!" (John 19:15). Jesus was being rejected by the very people he came to deliver. They had cried for his arrival, and they had prayed for him to come and deliver them. Now they were begging for Pilate to kill their Messiah.

Jesus was rejected by his own people for you and for me.

Pilate handed Jesus over to be crucified. Crucifixion was, according to the Jewish historian Josephus, "the most wretched of deaths." Jesus was on the cross for six hours. Dr. Truman Davis tells us what Christ experienced on the cross:

> As the arms fatigue, great waves of cramps sweep over the muscles, knotting them in deep, relentless, throbbing pain. With these cramps comes the inability to push Himself upward. Hanging by His arms, the pectoral muscles are paralyzed and the intercostal muscles are unable to act. Air can be drawn into the lungs, but cannot be exhaled. Jesus fights to raise Himself in order to get even one short breath. Finally, carbon dioxide builds up in the lungs and in the bloodstream and the cramps partially subside. Spasmodically, He is able to push Himself upward to exhale and bring in the life-giving oxygen.[4]

As he neared death Jesus was thirsty. A soldier placed a sponge soaked in wine vinegar to his lips. Jesus took a sip and then he said, "It is finished." He then bowed his head and died.

Jesus died on a cross for you and for me.

As I write this, I'm sitting in a room in Johnson City, Tennessee waiting for my van to be repaired. A television is on in the corner of the room. Three other people are waiting for their vehicles, too, but no one is talking or looking at each other. I'm working on my computer, and I just heard something on the TV that got my attention: eight U.S. soldiers were killed this morning by a car bomb in Baghdad, Iraq. The four of us look up, listen to the report, the guy on my right sighs … and life goes on. Does anybody care that eight young men were killed this morning? Do the Iraqis understand that these boys died trying to make them free? Will any Americans outside of their families and close friends shed a single tear for these boys today?

If we're honest, the deaths of strangers in distant lands don't mean too much to us.

To many of the people in this world, Jesus is a still a stranger who died in a distant land a long time ago, and they don't quite understand why his death really matters. They don't seem to understand that every human sins (see Rom. 3:23). They don't seem to understand that because of that sin we're all condemned to die (see Rom. 6:23). They don't seem to understand that God is just and must punish sin (see Rom. 3:25–26). He can't change his nature. If he did, we'd all be insecure not knowing what is right and what is wrong. They don't seem to understand that Christ was perfect (see Heb. 4:15). He never sinned, so he was an acceptable sacrifice for our sins. They don't seem to understand that God crucified Jesus for us. "God made him who had no sin to be sin for us, so that in him we might become the righteousness of God" (2 Cor. 5:21).

People don't understand because we haven't told them how much they are loved. Jesus was crucified because we are worth it.

"For God so loved the world that he gave his one and only Son, that whoever believes in him shall not perish but have eternal life" (John 3:16).

God loves the world. That means all of us. That means you. You are so valuable to God that he let his son die so that he could be with you forever.

Whenever you start to doubt your value to God just remember that Jesus got "owies" for you.

We must live lives worthy of such love.

FAITH

Stop doubting and believe.

—*John 20:27*

One hot summer day while vacationing in Florida, my wife, Rhonda, and her family were enjoying themselves in their hotel pool. Rhonda, who was always adventurous, noticed other kids going down the slide and decided to give it a try. Although she was little and not yet able to swim, her father assured her that he would catch her before she sank.

Rhonda climbed to the top of the slide and looked down at the pool. She was afraid. She had never been down the slide before, but her father had convinced her that she would love it. Rhonda yelled down to her father, "You'll catch me, right?"

"Yes dear, I'll catch you," her father replied.

With this reassurance, she slid into the pool, slipped through her father's arms, and went straight to the bottom. He dropped her.

Once more, Rhonda climbed to the top of the slide, and looked down upon the pool. She was really afraid. She had been down the slide and her father had dropped her. He had convinced her that she would love it, but he hadn't caught her. Rhonda yelled down to her father, "You'll catch me this time, right?"

"Yes, dear, I promise I'll catch you this time," her father replied—again.

Assured a second time, she slid into the pool, through her father's arms, and to the bottom of the pool. He dropped her—again.

Undaunted, Rhonda climbed to the top of the slide. She was terrified. Twice she had been dropped, but forgiving as she is, she gave her father one more chance.

"Dad, please catch me this time. Okay?"

"Yes dear, I promise I'll catch you this time."

You won't believe what happened. This is no lie—he dropped her again.

She was done with the slide for the day.

It's not fun to be dropped. It's a violation of trust.

Jesus told his disciples to trust him. "Do not let your hearts be troubled. Trust in God; trust also in me" (John 14:1). They were coming down the slide and expecting him to catch them. So to leave them now to stay dead in that tomb forever would have been catastrophic. It would have been like dropping them.

That didn't happen, though. Jesus didn't drop anyone.

Mary Magdelene went to the tomb and saw that the stone had been removed from the entrance. She ran to Simon Peter and said, "They have taken the Lord out of the tomb, and we don't know where they have put him!" (John 20:2). Peter and John ran to the tomb, but John reached the tomb first. When they looked inside they saw nothing except burial clothes.

One empty tomb; two clueless disciples. John wrote, "They still did not understand from Scripture that Jesus had to rise from the dead" (John 20:9). They probably wondered what to expect at the bottom of that steep slide.

Jesus caught Mary first. The disciples went back to their home, but Mary stood outside of the tomb and cried. Jesus showed up and spoke to Mary, but she thought he was the gardener ... until he spoke her name, "Mary" (John 20:16). There's just something about hearing your name spoken by one who loves you. Mary rushed back to the disciples shouting, "I have seen the Lord!"

Jesus then caught his disciples. They were gathered behind locked doors, afraid that the Jews would come for them next, when Jesus walked in through the door—I mean, he walked *through* the door!—and stood there. The first words out of his mouth were "Peace be with you!" Jesus always said the right thing at the right time. I know if I saw my formerly dead friend walking through the closed and locked door of my house, I might be a little uneasy. He figured they'd have some doubts about what they were seeing, so he showed them his pierced hands and side. They were overjoyed. He had caught them. He hadn't deserted them.

Finally, Jesus caught Thomas. Thomas was not with the other disciples, so he heard about Christ's appearing second hand. His reply: "I'll believe it when I see it." I think Thomas is unfairly criticized. Put yourself in his situation: You see Jesus executed on a cross, his body put in a tomb, a huge rock rolled in front of the tomb, and then you see the tomb guarded by Roman soldiers. It was not illogical for him to say, "Not even Jesus could come back from that" (my paraphrase). We now know the rest of the story; Thomas didn't. To label this guy Thomas "the Doubter" is to ignore the fact that he eventually believed.

Imagine if we labeled other people from the Bible by their lowest moment:

David "the Adulterer."

Aaron "the Idolater."

Paul "the Murderer."

Peter "the Denier."

Thomas just didn't want to be dropped like my wife was dropped by her father in the swimming pool, and I don't blame him.

He had spent three years with Jesus. He had followed Jesus

and had put his trust in him. He had also ministered with Jesus, so his heart told him that he had every reason to trust Jesus—but he had watched him die. He needed more.

I like Thomas. He owned his faith. Peter's faith wasn't enough for him. John's faith wasn't enough for him. Mary's faith wasn't enough for him. Thomas needed to believe for himself.

You must own your faith, too. Your grandparents may have been believers, and your parents may have been believers. Your spouse, siblings, children, and neighbors may all be believers, but Jesus won't be satisfied until you're a believer.

What's it going to take?

Do you need to speak to the Lord? Talk to him.

Do you need to hear from the Lord? Open up your Bible and let him speak to you.

Do you need to see the Lord? Open your eyes and look around at the beauty he's created in this world for you.

Do you need to feel the Lord? Open your heart in worship and allow him to calm your troubled soul. Let him touch you through his body—the church.

God wants you to have faith. He'll even meet you where you are. After all, Jesus made a special trip just for Thomas.

It happened one week later (see John 20:26). Did you get that? One week later. Jesus let Thomas think about it for a week. Have you been waiting for an answer from the Lord? Don't give up. Jesus always shows up at just the right time. Trust him.

Sure, Jesus could have appeared immediately to Thomas a week earlier and said, "Thomas, you whiner. Don't you know I'm busy? I have the world to save. Let's get this over with; touch me. Now get to work!" But he didn't. His timing was perfect.

The disciples were gathered in the same house and locked behind the same doors again, because they were still afraid. Jesus walked *through* the door (that's so cool!) and again said, "Peace be with you!" (John 20:26). He then looked straight at

Thomas and said, "Put your finger here; see my hands. Reach out your hand and put it into my side. Stop doubting and believe" (John 20:27).

Don't miss three important things about what Christ said:

First, Jesus knew exactly what proof Thomas needed to believe. How did Jesus know that a week earlier Thomas had said to the other disciples, "I need to touch his hands and side?" He knew because he was God.

Second, Jesus gave him exactly what he needed to believe. We may call it enabling, but God calls it love. Thomas didn't need a burning bush. Thomas didn't need the Red Sea to part. Thomas didn't need to be swallowed by a whale. He needed to touch Christ's hand and touch his side, so Jesus gave him what he needed.

Third, Jesus told him to stop doubting and believe. Enough already. There comes a time where we have to fish or cut bait. Jesus was counting on Thomas, and he needed to know if he was up for the task. Hot or cold? In or out? Believer or not?

Thomas, "the Doubter," morphed into Thomas, "the Believer," and cried out, "My Lord and my God!" (John 20:28).

We don't have Thomas' luxury. We are not going to be able to touch—or see—Jesus until he comes again, and by then it will be too late for the doubters. Jesus, burdened by that, spoke to you and me from behind those locked doors in that house in Jerusalem. He said to Thomas, "Because you have seen me, you have believed." To us he said, "Blessed are those who have not seen and yet have believed" (John 20:29). Jesus wants us to know that our faith can't be based only on what we see and touch. Faith based only on what we see and touch is not faith at all.

We are going to have to make a choice: we can choose to believe only what we see and touch, or we can believe in Jesus even though we can't see him. The first means Jesus can never be more to us than a man who lived a long time ago, a good teacher whose body is currently missing. We are alone on this planet to

◩ REFUEL!

1. Watch the movie Indiana Jones and the Last
Crusade, *featuring Harrison Ford.*
*2. In one of the last scenes of the movie, Indy Jones has
to pass several tests to save his father's life. Reflect on
what he had to do to get across the great chasm.*
*3. Would you have been willing to do what he did to
get across the chasm?*
*4. What was the key to his successful crossing of
the chasm?*
5. Would you have been able to do what he did?

fend for ourselves. There is nothing for us when we die except
the cold darkness of a pine box. Hope is only the wishful thinking of delusional people. The second means we can know the joy
of a personal relationship with the Creator of the universe, the
hope of a heavenly home when we die, and the promise of an
abundant life here on earth.

Do you want to have an abundant life? Then have faith. John
wrote, "Jesus did many other miraculous signs in the presence of
his disciples … But these are written that you may *believe* that
Jesus is the Christ, the Son of God, and that by *believing you may
have life* in his name" (John 20:30–31).

Faith in Jesus is life.

Do you believe?

Jump … he won't drop you.

COURAGE

As soon as Simon Peter heard him say, "It is the Lord," he wrapped his outer garment around him ... and jumped into the water.

—*John 21:7*

W e're born with only three fears: falling, loud noises, and bright light. We acquire the rest of our fears along the way.

I'm not afraid of them, but I know I definitely don't like tree frogs.

One night during the Olympics in Atlanta, I was up late watching highlights from the day's events at my sister and brother-in-law's house. As I watched, I noticed something jump into my field of vision. It was small, green, and slimy. I hate frogs. I watched it and carefully considered my options:

1. Try to catch it, but then I'd have to touch it. Not an option.
2. Try to chase it out, but risk waking up the whole house. Not an option.
3. Ignore it and act like I never saw it. What I did.

After it disappeared beneath the couch, I didn't give that frog another thought ... until three hours later.

It was about 3:00 in the morning. My wife, my two-year-old daughter, and I were sleeping on an air mattress on the floor in my sister's living room. In the fog of my slumber, I heard the following conversation:

My daughter: "Mommy, a frog just hopped on my face."

My wife: "Honey, just go back to sleep. It was just a dream."

Me: "No! It's not a dream! There's a frog in here!"

Immediately, every light in the house went on, and we frantically searched for the little green monster. My wife saved the day (or night?) when she put her extensive Tennessee-mountain-grown childhood experiences with frogs into action and snatched that creature "bald-headed" and threw him out the back door.

I came down from the highest point in the room and helped my wife restore order to the house.

The frog became a big deal when it didn't have to. I chose not to deal with it and ended up in the middle of a fiasco.

We all have things that frighten us: health problems, family problems, financial problems, and relationship problems.

We can choose to face these problems head on or ignore them and let them become more destructive. Ultimately, we need to be more courageous. We need to believe that "Greater is He who is in me, than He who is in the world." We need to be more like a llama.

Haven't you heard about llamas?

I read an interesting thing about llamas. Sheep farmers in the western United States have tried several things over time to keep coyotes from killing their sheep. The typical weapons were sprays, electric fences, "scare-coyotes," and even sleeping in the fields with their sheep. These were fine in the past, but now there's a new secret weapon—the llama.

Not that guy who sits cross-legged on the mountain top. The llama I'm referring to is the animal that looks like a camel without the humps.

In a field full of sheep, llamas don't appear to be afraid of anything. When they see something, they raise their head up and walk straight toward it. The coyotes see this aggressive behavior and want nothing to do with it. Coyotes are opportunists, and llamas take that opportunity away.

I like llamas. I want to be more like a llama. When I am afraid, I want to be more courageous.

Despite that denial thing, Peter was a pretty courageous guy. At the end of the book of John, we are able to witness a wonderful but often overlooked event. According to John 21, shortly after Christ's death, the disciples were having a rather unsuccessful fishing trip. In fact, the disciples weren't catching any fish. Jesus, standing on the shore and unrecognized by his disciples, shared his observation of their fishing trip. "Friends, haven't you any fish?" Thanks for the help!

Do you ever have days like that? We all face problems: We aren't catching any money. We aren't catching any health. We aren't catching any joy. We aren't catching any peace.

Jesus offered his advice. "Throw your net on the right side of the boat and you will find some." If you were a fisherman and you weren't catching any fish on the left side of the boat, would you think that it would change anything to fish on the right side of the boat? It sounds like stupid advice, but no advice is stupid when it comes from the maker of fish! The disciples listened to Jesus and threw their nets on the right side of the boat—and soon their nets were full.

I love Peter's reaction.

John recognized Jesus, "It is the Lord!" Peter heard what John said—just heard it—and that was enough for him. Peter put on his outer garment. Peter jumped in the water 100 yards from shore and began swimming to Jesus!

Don't miss the important lessons from this event:

- Jesus commands even the fish of the sea.
- Jesus knows a lot more than we do.
- Jesus wants the best for us.
- God's Word is true even to the smallest detail: 153 large fish!

But there's one more vital lesson I don't want you to miss:

Once you've lived, once you've walked on water, you'll sink if that's what it takes to be close to the One who gave you life.

Peter wasn't afraid of getting wet. He wasn't afraid of drowning. He wasn't afraid of rejection from the One he had rejected. In fact, from what we know from church history, Peter was courageous even to the point of his death during the reign of Nero. Peter had "Gotten a Life" and he never wanted to lose it again.

I pray that each person who spends time with this book will "Get a Life!" … and never want to lose it again.

Peter became a llama Christian. He walked through the rest of his life with courage and unwavering conviction. I want you to be a llama Christian, too. I want you to walk bravely toward the pain you are facing in life. I want you to walk bravely toward the fear that has tried to paralyze you. It feels good to be so full of life that you walk bravely, even in the face of death. When you do, you'll see it turn tail and run off for all eternity.

So repeat after me:

"I will not be afraid."

"I will be brave."

"Jesus brought life into my world."

"Jesus conquered death on the cross."

"I am victorious through the blood of Jesus!"

"I am not a loser!"

"I am a winner!"

"I am not dead!"

"I am alive!"

"I will be a llama Christian!"

Doesn't that feel good?

God wants you to feel empowered in this life. Jesus didn't die on a cross so that you and I would die. He came so that you and I would fully live. Don't desecrate Christ's sacrifice by cowering in the face of Satan's attacks. Live like a llama.

◰ REFUEL!

1. Get a pencil and a piece of paper, and list your three greatest fears.

2. Erase your three greatest fears and over the place where they were list your three favorite promises from God.

3. Next time you see a llama, say "Thanks."

LEAVE THE LOCKER ROOM!

◩

I remember the smells, the feelings, and the speeches. Locker rooms are important for success in team sports. A locker room is a place where focus is restored, errors are corrected, mistakes are confronted, and the team is encouraged.

Locker rooms are interesting places. They also are smelly places. If you haven't been in a locker room, take my word for it. Some guys have superstitions about washing their clothes. In fact, I played a whole season without washing my practice uniform, which wasn't really that big of a deal since I rarely played. I was six feet three, and soaking wet with all my clothes on still weighed only 155 pounds. Occasionally, I would hold up both arms and stand in for the goalposts.

In a locker room, guys talk loudly and coaches grunt loudly. At some point before game time, the coach's grunting would get more intense and we, his players, would get worked into a frenzy.

Now athletes all have different pregame rituals: Some sit and stare, some hit their head against the locker, and some put headphones on. It's an exciting place. You can hear the band playing, you can hear the crowds gathering, and you can hear the cheerleaders cheering. When you are in the locker room, you can't wait to come running out through the banner and onto the field. But the game is not won in the locker room, the fun is not in the locker room, and the victory is not won in the locker room.

If the coach has done his job well, the team will leave the locker room committed to doing whatever it takes to win the game. I have been in many locker rooms, and it has never crossed my mind to stay in there during the game. It would be pointless. Victory is not found in the locker room but in the arena of competition. Losers live in locker rooms.

I am afraid that many people have developed a locker-room mentality. Too many people have built a home in their comfort zone and have forgotten the "game"—life—outside.

I grew up thinking about victory. In fact, some of my earliest memories have to do with victory, and my life was eternally scarred. You see, both of my older sisters were cheerleaders.

Let me give you a brief sample of what I heard growing up:

"We've got spirit yes we do."

"Be Aggressive. Be, Be Aggressive. B-E-AGG-RESS-IVE!"

"RE-REB-REBOUND. Miss it. Rebound. Miss it. Rebound.

"V-I-C-T-O-R-Y. Victory is our battle cry."

"M-I-S-S-I-T-R-E-B-O-U-N-D. Miss it. Rebound."

(With all of the spelling they do, it seems that cheerleaders are "hooked on phonics.")

But the worst cheer of all time was, "That's all right, that's okay. We're gonna beat you anyway!" I once heard this cheer from our cheerleaders in junior high when our team was down 70-0 with one minute to go in the game. That was not "okay!" It was hopeless. We were going to lose.

But friend, let me cheer you on. Your life is not hopeless.

You may be suffocating in fear.

You may be blinded by discouragement.

You may be stumbling through sickness.

But don't give up! Don't quit! Don't be a loser!

Keep playing the game of life.

No matter how bad it seems, with God's help we can overcome. No matter how great the challenge seems, we can make it through. No matter how big the mountain, we can climb it. No matter how bad the odds seem, we can win. No matter the enemy we are facing, we must stand and proclaim, "That's all right. That's okay. We're going to beat you anyway."

It will take work to win, though. We must fight our tendency to laziness. As a people, we have become so lazy. We have gift bags, remote control (We will tear apart the entire house to find it just so we don't have to get up and turn the channel.), instant food, one-day diets, instant oil changes, instant grits (there are some things that should not be instant), and ATMs. We will drive around and around the parking lot for an hour, so we can have a space by the front door.

It will take risk to win.

In the locker room you will never get tackled.

In the locker room you will never get muddy.

In the locker room you will never miss a tackle.

In the locker room you will never drop a ball.

But ...

In the locker room you will never make a tackle.

In the locker room you will never make a big play.

In the locker room you will never hear the roar of the crowd.

In the locker room you will never score a touchdown.

In the locker room you will never win a game.

We must get out of the comfort zone and play the game.

During Matt Simon's first year as head football coach at the University of North Texas in Denton, the team was one of the smallest and slowest in the Southland Conference. When the McNeese State team took the field for a pregame warm-up, the UNT players were totally intimidated by the size of their opponents from Louisiana. But in the locker room before the game, Simon gave his team a rousing speech and they stormed powerfully onto the field, eager to play. Later, an alumnus asked Simon what he had said to motivate his players. The coach confessed, "I simply told them that the last eleven guys out this locker-room door to the field had to start the game."

During a *Monday Night Football* game between the Chicago Bears and the New York Giants, one of the commentators observed that Walter Payton had accumulated over nine miles in career rushing yardage. The other remarked, "Yeah, and that's with someone knocking you down every 4.6 yards."

Viktor Frankl, the Austrian psychiatrist and Holocaust survivor, wrote in his book *Man's Search for Meaning* that one of the most demeaning and damaging aspects of life in concentration camps was the assignment of deliberately meaningless tasks, such as moving piles of dirt endlessly from one site to another for no purpose at all. "I can survive any 'how' as long as there is a 'why,'" Frankl wrote.

We have a purpose in this world. We must find it and be unafraid to fulfill it.

Legend tells of a time that Knute Rockne, the head football coach at the University of Notre Dame, was about to face the football team from the University of Southern California, and knew it was a far superior team. He wondered if there was any way he could defeat them. Then he hit on an idea. He scoured the city of South Bend, Indiana for about a hundred of the biggest men he could find. When he had about a hundred men, each at least six foot five and weighing in at three hundred pounds or more, he put them all in Notre Dame uniforms. With the shoulder pads and the helmets, they looked even bigger. Then, when it was time for the game to begin, he sent these men out of the locker room first. As the USC team watched, they just kept coming and coming and coming until these hundred men were all the USC team saw. The USC coach kept telling his team, "They can only field eleven men at a time." But the damage was done. None of these men ever played one minute of the game. But USC had become so intimidated at the sight of them that they were unable to function, and Notre Dame won the game.

Friend, face your fears, confront your doubts, find the strength to get into life's game, and play like a winner.

Recently, my daughter announced to her mother and me that she wanted to be a cheerleader. Yippee. But the truth is, I'm proud that she's choosing to be a part of life's game. That's something even I can cheer about.

◩ REFUEL!

1. Go to a local trophy store and buy a small (or large, depending on how much encouragement you need) trophy and have the following engraved:

(YOUR NAME)
LEFT THE LOCKER ROOM
(DATE*)

* (This is the date you "left the locker room."
Obviously, you must "leave the locker room" before
you can date the trophy.)

2. Display this trophy in the place in your world where you feel the most defeated.

3. Do something today that requires courage.

4. Get a Bible, turn to the last two pages, and read Revelation 21 and 22. We win!

Notes

INTRODUCTION

1. I heard Calvin Miller say this phrase during a presentation at the 1997 Annual Conference of North American Professors of Christian Education.
2. This song is entitled, "Life Goes On." It was a song my sister wrote for our family. It was never published.

ELEMENT 2: PURITY

1. Ezekiel was most likely written between 590–570 BC, and Revelation is thought to have been written about AD 96. John sees a vision of the temple "filled with smoke from the glory of God" in Revelation 15:8.

ELEMENT 3: NEWNESS

1. My daughter Payton arrived according to God's plan, which once again involved arriving at the hospital in the middle of the night. God is good … and consistent.

ELEMENT 4: WORSHIP

1. Quote taken from the "Premise" posted on Matthew Alper's Web site: http://www.godpart.com.

ELEMENT 5: GROWTH

1. Leonard Sweet, *Soul Tsunami* (Grand Rapids: Zondervan Publishing House, 1999), 84.

ELEMENT 6: RETREAT

1. John Ortberg, *The Life You've Always Wanted* (Grand Rapids: Zondervan Publishing House, 2002), 83.

ELEMENT 7: DISCERNMENT

1. Survey of 6,000 people polled in 1988, *U.S. News and World Report,* Jan. 30, 1989.
2. James Dobson, *Bringing Up Boys* (Wheaton, Ill.: Tyndale House Publishers, 2001), 91–92.

ELEMENT 9: VISION

1. Max Lucado, *God Came Near* (Sisters, Ore.: Multnomah Press, 1987), 13.
2. Prevent Blindness America, "Eye Problems," http://www.preventblindness.org/eye_problems/eye_problems.html.

ELEMENT 11: TRANSFORMATION

1. This article was posted on cbsnews.com on the "Odd Truth" page on February 20, 2004.
2. In John 10:40 we read that Jesus had crossed the Jordan from Jerusalem. In Roman times, the area east of the Jordan River between the Sea of Galilee and the Dead Sea and south of the Decapolis was called Peraea.
3. This quote comes from an article in the Associated Press about the same incident. "Funeral Home Head Finds Live Body," The Associated Press, Thursday, Jan. 25, 2001; 6:54 AM EST, Ashland, Mass.

ELEMENT 13: SERVICE

1. My friend Mark Moore said this in a sermon on the topic of service at the Florida State Christian Convention in Tarpon Springs, Florida in September 2003.
2. *The Commission,* June 2002, 26.

ELEMENT 14: FOCUS

1. For a link to the complete list, go to my Web site: www.arronchambers.com; *The Phobia List*.

2. Cheryl Wetzstein, "Fatherless Homes No Longer on Rise," *Washington Times*, April 9, 2002; Wade F. Horn and Tom Sylvester, *Father Facts*, 4th ed., 2002, National Fatherhood Initiative.

3. "My Mommy Comes Back," *Baby Songs*, Backyard Enterprises, Inc., Troy, Michigan, 1993.

ELEMENT 15: FRUIT

1. Merrill C. Tenney, *John: The Gospel of Belief* (Grand Rapids: Wm. B. Eerdmans Publishing Co., 1948), 227–28.

ELEMENT 16: PEACE

1. Moody Bible Institute, "Today In The Word," June 19, 1992, http://www.todayintheword.org/GenMoody.

2. Charles F. Kettering as quoted in *Bits and Pieces Magazine*, December 1991, 24.

ELEMENT 17: PRAYER

1. This quote comes from an online report on the story dated August, 13, 2001 on the Web site: www.abcnews.go.com.

2. Weldon M. Hardenbrook, *Missing from Action: Vanishing Manhood in America* (Nashville: Thomas Nelson Co., 1987).

ELEMENT 18: HOMESICKNESS

1. Stanley Hauerwas and William H. Willimon, *Resident Aliens: A provocative Christian assessment of culture and ministry for people who know that something is wrong* (Nashville: Abingdon Press, 1989), 12.

ELEMENT 19: VALUE

1. Josh McDowell, *A Ready Defense* (San Bernardino, Calif.: Here's Life Publishers, Inc., 1990), 222.
2. Ibid., 222.
3. Ibid., 222.
4. Ibid., 224.

Readers' Guide

For Personal Reflection
or Group Discussion

Readers' Guide

◩

I hope this book has motivated you to live a more abundant life. I hope that you will begin to implement each of the twenty-one elements in your life right now. And I do mean *right now*. Don't wait.

Sometimes, with good intentions, we justify mediocrity today with empty words promising excellence tomorrow.

"I'll go on a diet after the holidays."

"I'll go back and finish school later."

"I'm going to stop smoking soon."

"Daddy's busy right now. I'll play catch with you tomorrow."

Sometimes Satan uses the promise of tomorrow to choke the life out of today's promises. Satan doesn't like positive change. He doesn't want you to have a more abundant life, so he'll try to convince you to change your life tomorrow knowing that tomorrow never comes for most people.

This book is a call for you to walk with Jesus down the narrow path "that leads to life" (Matt. 7:14). Jesus calls it "narrow" to let us know that it's going to be difficult to walk this path, but it isn't impossible. We can do it. You can do it. You can have a more abundant life today.

This discussion guide is designed to help you "Get a life" by moving the elements of an abundant life off of the pages of this book and into your present reality. As you work through these questions, reading and studying through the entire book of John and implementing the "Big Ideas" along the way, it's my prayer that God will help you to see each element as valuable and attainable.

Blessings, life-getter.

Element 1—Light

Personal Reflection: Do this study in a dark closet or outside at night with a flashlight.

Group Discussion: You might want to dim the lights or turn them out altogether for this particular study to help create a teachable moment. If you plan on turning the lights out, ask your members to come equipped with flashlights.

1. Were you afraid of the dark when you were a child?

2. If you were, what in particular about the darkness frightened you?

3. If you were not, what in particular kept you from being afraid?

At this point, read through John 1.

4. Does Jesus want us to be afraid and trapped in darkness? What in John 1 supports your answer?

5. How has your relationship with the "Light of the World"—Jesus—brightened your world?

6. What are you going to do this week to share the "Light of the World" with someone else?

7. Prayer Starter: *"Lord, make me a light in this dark world."*

Element 2—Purity

Personal Reflection: Get really dirty before doing this study and bathe as soon as you are finished.

Group Study: At the end of your lesson, give each participant a wrapped or boxed bar of soap. Ask your members to write one thing they will do to maintain purity in their lives on their soap box or wrapper.

1. Can you remember a time in your life when your body was really dirty? What caused the filth? What did it take to get clean?

2. Think about a time in your life when you looked your best? What was the situation? In your life, has it been easier to get dirty or stay clean? Explain you answer.

At this point, read through John 2.

3. Why was Jesus so angry when he found men selling sheep and doves and exchanging money in the temple?

4. Share something that you would not allow in your house. Why not?

5. In 1 Corinthians 3:16 Paul wrote, "Don't you know that you yourselves are God's temple and that God's Spirit lives in you?" How should knowing that Christians are temples of the Holy Spirit impact our lives?

6. Share or list three things you can do this week to clean up your temple.

7. Prayer Starter: *"Lord, purify this temple and make me strong in the face of sin."*

ELEMENT 3—NEWNESS

Personal Reflection: Look at your baby pictures or watch a video of your birth before this study.

Group Study: Ask each member to bring a baby picture to the study. As each member arrives, collect the pictures and arrange them on a table with corresponding numbered Post-It notes. Play a game in which the members try to identify which adult goes with which baby picture.

1. When you think about childbirth what is the first word that comes to mind (Men's and women's answers may vary.)? What are some of the biggest misconceptions (pardon the choice of words) about childbirth?

2. Share some of the emotions that childbirth evokes. Why?

At this point, read through John 3.

3. How is being "born again" as a Christian like actual childbirth?

4. How should the image of conversion as a birth impact how new Christians are treated by other Christians? What can mature Christians do to help new Christians mature in their faith?

5. What can you do to help other people to be "born again"?

6. Prayer Starter: *"Lord, use me to share salvation with those who need the hope of eternal life."*

ELEMENT 4—WORSHIP

Personal Reflection: After you finish this Bible study, get a bottle of water. With a fine-tipped marker, write words on the bottle that represent reasons you have to worship God.

Group Study: At the end of your Bible study, give each group member a bottle of water and a fine-tipped marker. Ask each person to write words on the bottle that represent reasons he has to worship God. This should be kept as a reminder to worship God.

1. What is your favorite thing about worship at your church? What is your least favorite thing about worship? If you could change one thing about worship, what would it be? Why?

2. What are the biggest barriers between you and worship of God? What best prepares you for worship?

At this point, read through John 4.

3. Share several of the "wells" you find yourself most tempted to drink from during the week. Why are these "wells" so appealing?

4. How has your worship of God impacted your spiritual life?

5. Finish this statement: I want to worship God better, so I will …

6. Prayer Starter: *"Lord, I want to worship you and only you."*

ELEMENT 5—GROWTH

Personal Reflection: Buy a red and blue kindergarten nap mat. After reading this lesson, list your goals for the next ten years on the red side of the mat. On the blue side, write, Pick up your mat and walk!

Group Study: Ask each member to bring a copy of his or her school yearbook. During the lesson, give each member a chance to explain how she has changed since the picture was taken.

1. What are your most important accomplishments? Briefly share what you had to do to achieve these accomplishments.

2. Share five goals you have for your life. What are you willing to do to reach these goals?

3. What obstacles do you think you will have to overcome to accomplish these goals?

At this point, read through John 5.

    4. Are you like the paralytic? If so, in what ways?

    5. What has Jesus helped you to accomplish that you would not have been able to accomplish alone?

    6. Prayer Starter: *"Lord, I want to walk. Help me to do what you have made me to do."*

ELEMENT 6—RETREAT

Personal Reflection: Go off by yourself for this study. A quiet place outside would be perfect.

Group Study: As you begin this lesson, ask the group to retreat with you to a solitary place outside. As you lead this lesson, allow time for quiet reflection.

    1. What are the top three biggest distractions in your life?

    2. Share the last time you were alone for an extended period of time (in bed asleep does not count!). What impact did this time have on your life?

At this point, read through John 6.

    3. What are the biggest obstacles to your time of personal retreat with the Lord?

    4. Are these obstacles truly urgent or just important? What's the difference?

    5. What can you do to create time of personal retreat with the Lord?

    6. Prayer Starter: *"Lord, help me to know when to retreat."*

ELEMENT 7—DISCERNMENT

Personal Reflection: Before you begin this study, get your calendar and review the past year. Answer this question: "Based on what is on this calendar, what were my priorities last year?"

Group Study: Ask your group members to bring their personal planning calendars or personal data assistants (PDA) with them to this study.

    1. As you think about everything you did over the past year, what are the top three things that monopolized your time?

2. How closely do these activities align with your priorities?

3. What keeps us from doing what we really need to be doing? What can we do to remove these obstacles?

At this point, read through John 7.

4. What do we learn about priorities from the example of Jesus in this passage?

5. Pull out your calendar. Share one thing you are going to remove from or add to your calendar so that you will "be where the bein' is."

6. Prayer starter: *"Lord, help me to be where the bein' is."*

ELEMENT 8—HOPE

Personal Reflection: Find a picture of someone in your life who is one of your biggest heroes.

Group Study: Ask the members of your small group to each come with a picture of one of the heroes of their lives. Before this study begins, ask the members to share why their heroes are their heroes.

1. Who is one of the biggest heroes of your life? Why?

2. What makes a hero?

3. Were you ever bullied as a child? How did that make you feel?

At this point, read through John 8.

4. Based on this event and Jesus' teachings in the gospels, what is Jesus willing to do to protect those who are being picked on by bullies?

5. How has Jesus been your hero? Be specific.

6. What can you do to be someone's hero this week?

7. Prayer starter: *"Lord, thank you for being my hero. Help me to be someone's hero this week."*

ELEMENT 9—VISION

Personal Reflection: Begin this lesson without your contacts in or your glasses on. Reflect on how it feels to be unable to see.

Group Study: Prior to your group's arrival, put up an eye chart on a wall in your house. Before you start your lesson, "test" the vision of each member of your group. You may want to make this a little more fun by giving the person with the worst vision a pair of cheap bifocals.

At this point, read through John 9.

1. Close your eyes for 2 minutes (no peeking!). Was that uncomfortable? Why? What was it like to open your eyes for the first time? What was the first thing you wanted to see?

2. Reflect on blindness. What would you miss seeing the most?

3. What is blinding you now?

4. Stop and look around this room. List three things you've never noticed before.

   a)
   b)
   c)

   Why do you think you've never really seen these things before? What can you do to have better vision?

5. Prayer Starter: *"Lord, I want to see you. I want to see people the way you see them. I want to see this world with your eyes. I want to see your visions and your dreams fulfilled in my life. Protect my eyes from spiritual blindness. Help me to recognize those things in my life that are hazardous to my vision."*

ELEMENT 10—SUBMISSION

Personal Reflection: Is there a farm or a zoo nearby? If so, go through this lesson in the presence of some submissive animals. Reflect on the blessings they receive from their providers.

Group Study: Here are a couple of ideas: 1) At some point in the lesson, play a game of "Simon Says." Reflect on how well we listen and follow orders. 2) Before you start the lesson, read off a list of "New Group Rules." Act serious as you list the rules that everyone must follow from then on. The more legalistic you can make the rules, the better. After reading the list, ask the group how they felt as they were listening to the rules being read off.

1. Share a time when you got into trouble as a child. What were the details? How did you feel when you were being punished? How do you feel about that punishment now?

2. Do you have a hard time with submission? Why?

3. Which laws are the hardest for you to obey? Why?

At this point, read through John 10.

4. Share some of the blessings you've received from Jesus, the Good Shepherd.

5. What is God's will for your life?

6. What do you need to change in order to submit to God's will?

7. Prayer Starter: *"Lord, you are the boss of me. I trust you and will follow you wherever you lead me. I know that you know my name. I know you know me better than anyone else. You love me, and you are leading me to a safe place. Lord, help me hear your voice through the noise of my daily life. Lord, give me the courage to follow you even when I can't see where we are going. Lord, protect me from the thief, and help me to be able to discern his voice from yours. I want an abundant life, so help me to submit to your will."*

ELEMENT 11—TRANSFORMATION

Personal Reflection: Find two pictures of yourself, one when you were a child and one that's more current. How have you changed over the years? Be specific.

Group Study: Ask the members of your group to bring pictures of themselves as children and pictures taken more recently. Begin the lesson by asking the group members to show each type of picture. The physical changes are obvious, so ask each member to describe the biggest change he or she has experienced that cannot be seen.

1. If you could change one thing about yourself, what would it be? Why?

2. What typically keeps us from making positive changes in our lives?

At this point, read through John 11.

3. When Jesus arrived at Lazarus's tomb, he cried. What does this tell us about Jesus?

4. Read and reflect on the following Scriptures:

> Therefore, I urge you, brothers, in view of God's mercy, to offer your bodies as living sacrifices, holy and pleasing to God— this is your spiritual act of worship. Do not conform any longer to the pattern of this world, but be transformed by the renewing of your mind. Then you will be able to test and approve what God's will is—his good, pleasing and perfect will. (Rom. 12:1–2)

> Now the Lord is the Spirit, and where the Spirit of the Lord is, there is freedom. And we, who with unveiled faces all reflect the Lord's glory, are being transformed into his likeness with ever-increasing glory, which comes from the Lord, who is the Spirit. (2 Cor. 3:17–18)

5. According to these Scriptures, what tools will God use to lead us through transformation?

6. Prayer starter: *"Lord, transform me."*

ELEMENT 12—PASSION

Personal Reflection: Find an object that represents one of your passions. Hold this item as you begin this study.

Group Study: Ask each group member to bring an item to the study that represents something he is passionate about. During this study, ask him to explain his passion.

1. What are you passionate about? Share (or write) your top three passions in life:

2. Which one of the passions you shared (or listed) has made your life important?

3. Which one of the passions you shared (or listed) has made your life impactful?

At this point, read through John 12.

4. Read John 12:1–11 and finish these statements. Write your answers below.

a. Lord, forgive me for wasting passion on the following things:

b. Lord, because I'm passionate about you I will give you the following:

c. Lord, because I'm passionate about people I will do this today:

d. Reflecting on your answers, is there anything you noted above that you would like to share with the group?

5. (This is optional, but can give your study more impact. You will need to make sure every member of the study brings his or her checkbook to the group study. This activity would work for Personal Reflection as well.) Mary's passion for God drove her to pour perfume on Jesus' feet. This perfume was worth a year's wages. Think about how much money you make in a year. How would it feel to give that much money to God? Let's find out!

a. Get your checkbook and open it.
b. Make a check out to God.
c. The amount of the check should be equivalent to what you make in a year. *How did that feel?*
d. On the memo line write: *Not a waste!*
e. Sign the check.
f. Hold the check and pray this prayer as a group:

Lord, this represents my passion for you. You are everything to me, so I give you everything. You are the best, so I give you my best. Thank you for not thinking that it was a waste to send your Son to die for me. Lord, use my passion for you as a tool to change my life and the lives of people around me. Make my life important for you. Make my life have impact for your glory. Lord, help me to be passionate about you and passionate about your people. Amen.

g. Open your Bible to John 12 and place this check there as a bookmark and a reminder of your passion for God.

6. Prayer Starter: *"Lord, because I'm passionate about you, I will ..."*

ELEMENT 13—SERVICE

Personal Reflection: Do this study in the lobby of a local nursing home, hospital, or soup kitchen, and reflect on its meaning to you afterward.

Group Study: Build this study around a special meal and foot-washing ceremony. This needs to be done with a group of people with whom you can be vulnerable. All you will need is a large bowl, towels, and water pitcher.

1. After everyone has arrived and eaten together, read John 13:1–17.

2. Lead the group in a time of foot washing. As each member washes someone's feet, encourage her to tell the person whose feet she is washing something she admires about her. This may take a while and you won't want to rush this, so allow enough time.

3. How did it feel to wash someone else's feet? What thoughts ran through your mind?

4. How did it feel to have your feet washed? What thoughts ran through your mind?

5. If you could only wash one person's feet, whose would they be and why?

6. Read this prayer as a group asking the group to repeat each line after you.

> *Lord, we know that you put all things under Christ's power.*
> *Lord, we know that Jesus came from you.*
> *Lord, we know that Jesus returned back to you after his resurrection.*
> *Lord, we know that unless you wash us we have no part in you.*
> *Lord, we know and understand what you have done for us.*
> *Lord, we know that you are our Teacher.*
> *Lord, we know that you are our Lord.*
> *Lord, we know that you want us to serve each other.*
> *Please help us to serve each other as you served us.*
> *Lord, we know these things …*
> *And we know that we will be blessed if we do them.*
> *Amen.*

ELEMENT 14—FOCUS

Personal Reflection: Get a blank piece of paper and some crayons before you start this study.

Group Study: As your group members arrive, give each one a box of crayons and a blank piece of paper.

1. What issues are troubling your heart right now? Share or list the top three below:

   a)

   b)

   c)

2. What's your biggest fear as you think about the future? List it here:
_____phobia

At this point, read through John 14.

3. What's the first image that pops into your mind when you think about heaven?

4. What do you look forward to the most when you think about heaven?

5. What will you miss the least about life here on earth?

6. When was the last time you colored? It's been too long, I'm sure. Using only crayons, draw a picture of the mansion waiting for you in heaven. Share your picture with the rest of the group. After this study, hang this picture someplace where you will see it often, like your refrigerator or your bathroom mirror. Each time you see this picture, focus your troubled heart on your heavenly home.

7. Pray Starter: *"Lord, my heart has been troubled by* _____. *(Be specific about what is troubling your heart. Remember that God is big enough to handle your pain.) I trust you, I love you, and I put my hope in you. You are my Father today, and you'll be my Father forever. Thank you for preparing a big, beautiful home for me in heaven. Lord, please focus my troubled heart on home."*

ELEMENT 15—FRUIT

Personal Reflection: Before beginning this study, get a piece of your favorite fruit. After this study, eat the fruit.

Group Study: As each group member arrives, give him a piece of fruit.

1. What is your favorite fruit? Why?

At this point, read through John 15.

2. Why do you think Jesus compares our good works to fruit?

3. According to John 15:4, what is the key to bearing fruit?

4. What are the consequences for not bearing fruit? Why are the consequences so severe?

5. Read Galatians 5:16–26. In this passage, Paul identifies both the fruit of the sinful nature and the fruit of the Spirit. Of the fruits of the Spirit, which one is the hardest for you to consistently produce?

6. Prayer Starter: *"Lord, you are the vine and I am one of your branches. I need you. I will die without you. Prune me and prepare me to bear fruit. Help me to stay connected to you. Show me what my life would be like without you so that I will never cut myself off from you. Father, I want to be fruitful. I want to be a blessing to this world for you and your glory. Lord, help me to show myself to be one of your disciples."*

ELEMENT 16—PEACE

Personal Reflection: Before you begin this study, get a copy of today's newspaper. Highlight or circle any article that has anything to do with war or conflict. Reflect on what you found.

Group Study: As you begin this lesson, distribute copies of newspapers and news magazines to the group. Give the members fifteen minutes to cut out every article that has anything to do with war or conflict. Discuss your results.

1. Share or list the top three battles you are fighting at this time of your life.

a)

b)

c)

2. What keeps you from being overwhelmed in the face of these conflicts?

3. What "weapons" do you find most useful as you fight these battles?

At this point, read through John 16.

4. What battles did the disciples have to fight?

5. Why would Jesus' description of the work of the Holy Spirit be encouraging to the disciples?

6. In what ways does the Holy Spirit help you fight the battles in your life?

7. Prayer Starter: *"Lord, Prince of Peace, help me to be an instrument of your peace in this world of wars."*

ELEMENT 17—PRAYER

Personal Reflection: If you had only one night left to live, what would you do? Where would you go? What would you pray? Get a piece of paper and write a prayer to God as if this were the last prayer of your life on earth.

Group Study: Sometime during the week before this study, ask the group members to write a prayer as if it were the last prayer of their lives on earth.

1. Share a time when God answered one of your prayers. What lessons did you learn from this experience?

2. Do you have a good prayer life? If not, share or list the top 3 barriers to your prayer life.

    a)
    b)
    c)

At this point, read through John 17.

3. As you think about Jesus' prayer in John 17, what barriers did he have to overcome as he prayed?

4. This week you wrote a prayer as if it were the last prayer of your life on earth. Please share your prayer with the group.

5. How is this prayer different from the prayers you typically pray?

6. Prayer Starter: *"Lord, thank you for allowing me to communicate with you like this. Here's what's on my heart...."*

ELEMENT 18—HOMESICKNESS

Personal Reflection: Go to the nearest office supply store and buy a globe. After finishing this study, get a marker and write on the globe in large letters, Not my home. Keep this globe in a place where you can look at it and think of your real home.

Group Study: Before this study, buy a globe. During this study, ask each member to point out where she was born and where she'd like to visit before she dies and why. At the end of the lesson, ask each person to write on the globe, Not my home.

1. What are your favorite things about life on earth?

2. What are your least favorite things about life on earth?

3. When you think about heaven, what are you most looking forward to?

At this point, read through John 18.

4. Share or list the specific forms of rejection Jesus experienced in this chapter from the citizens of this world. How would you have responded to this treatment?

5. This chapter deals with denials and trials. Which of these would have been the hardest for you to endure?

6. Prayer Starter: *"Lord, I know you've sent me here for a reason. This world is not my home. Use me to make a difference here. Keep me from getting too comfortable here. Make me homesick for heaven, while also making me passionate for lost people here on earth. Thanks for entrusting this mission to me. I'll be home soon."*

Element 19—Value

Personal Reflection: Before you begin this study, get a box of Band-Aids, a red fine-tip marker, and a white piece of paper. Draw a picture of a cross on the piece of paper. At the end of this lesson, pray this prayer: "Lord, I am a sinner. I love you and I know that you love me. You sent Jesus to die for my sins. I repent of my sins. Lord, please forgive me of...." (Confess your sins, naming each one specifically. As you confess a sin, write the specific sin on a Band-Aid with a marker and stick it on the cross.)

Group Study: Before this study, nail two pieces of wood (preferably two inches by four inches) together in the form of a cross. Get a red fine-tip marker and a box of Band-Aids. At the end of this lesson, ask each member to write one sin he'd like to confess on the white side of the Band-Aid. After prayer, ask each person to stick his Band-Aids to the cross. You might want to close this part of your study by singing "Amazing Grace."

1. What's the hardest experience you've had to endure in your life?

2. What got you through that difficult time?

At this point, read through John 19.

3. Describe the first time you really understood what Jesus did for you on the cross.

4. Read 2 Corinthians 5:11–21. According to this passage, who crucified Jesus? Why was he crucified?

5. Share one thing you will do this week because of what you've remembered, or learned, about crucifixion.

6. Prayer Starter: *"Lord, thank you for forgiving me of my sins. Jesus, thank you for dying for my sins. I love you. I will live a life worthy of your sacrifice."*

ELEMENT 20—FAITH

Personal Reflection: Before you begin this study, get a chair from your kitchen or dining room. Sit down. Why did you trust the chair to support your weight? How is this like faith in God?

Group Study: Before you begin this study, take turns blindfolding a person and having him or her walk through and around some obstacles while listening to the commands of another person. After everyone has had an opportunity, ask the group to share how they felt having to put their trust in one person.

1. If you were labeled by your lowest point in life, what would be your name? (i.e. John "the Candy-stealer," Suzie "the Partier," etc.)

2. If you were labeled by your life right now, what would your name be?

3. If you could pick a name for yourself, what would it be?

At this point, read through John 20.

4. Share a time when you did something that required a lot of faith. What did you learn from that experience?

5. Share or reflect on the time when you first put your faith in Christ Jesus. What led you to finally believe in him?

6. Do you believe that Jesus Christ is the Son of God? If so, I want you to write your creed. (Leaders: Please provide a piece of paper and a pencil for each member.) A creed is a statement of faith which summarizes what one believes. I want you to get a nice piece of paper (suitable for framing) and write out what you believe concerning God, the Holy Spirit, Jesus, the Bible, etc. (You can find sample creeds on my web site: www.arronchambers.com.) Once you have completed your creed, I'd like you to frame it and place it where you—and others—can see it.

7. Prayer Starter: Close your devotional time by praying your creed saying, *"Lord, I believe...."*

ELEMENT 21—COURAGE

*Personal Reflection: Conduct this study in the food court of a local shopping mall.
And—yes—you'll need to take your Bible with you! At the end of this study, reflect
on how it felt to live your faith in a public arena.*

*Group Study: Want to do something slightly courageous but not life-threatening?
Why not conduct this study around tables in the food court of a local shopping mall
(Yes—with Bibles and prayer, too!)? Your members will get a taste of what it feels like
to do something slightly risky. If you want to do something even more courageous,
end this study by giving your members an hour to mill around the mall with the
vision of having at least one conversation with someone about Christ. Meet back in
the food court and share your stories.*

1. Share or reflect on a time when you had to be courageous.

At this point, read through John 21.

2. What is the most courageous thing you've ever done for Jesus?

3. What prompted your courageous act?

4. In this chapter, Jesus shows his power as God's Son in several ways.
   Can you identify three actions that show Jesus is God?

5. How should knowing that Jesus is God impact the choices we make
   in life?

6. What is the significance of John 21:24?

7. What is the significance of John 21:25?

8. You've now finished reading the entire gospel of John. In this gospel,
   you've been reminded that Jesus Christ is truly God's Son. Share one
   thing you will do this week because of that knowledge.

9. Prayer Starter: *"Lord, I know that you love me and I know that you are God.
   Because I believe these facts, I will ..."*